microwave cooking library®

microwaving light & healthy

by barbara methven

microwave cooking library®

For years Americans paid attention to their diet only when they wanted to lose weight. In the past decade interest has been growing in honest nutrition as an aid to health and fitness.

People are beginning to check food labels for high sodium and sugar content and are reducing the fats, sugars and salt used in home cooking. They're learning to enjoy lean poultry and fish, and are eating less red meat. They increase the fiber in their diet with vegetables, fruits and whole grains.

Microwave oven owners who want to cook for health and fitness have a head start. Chicken, fish and vegetables are among the foods the microwave oven cooks best. Microwaving is naturally low-fat, and it brings out the flavor of foods so you can reduce salt. Tender-crisp microwaved vegetables retain their vitamins and useful fiber.

This book is designed to help you make the most of the microwave advantage. You'll find plenty of variety to provide all the nutrients you need daily. You'll learn that nutritious doesn't mean dull. What's good for you can be just plain good.

Barbara Methven

Barbara Methven

CREDITS:
Design & Production: Cy DeCosse Incorporated
Consultant: Joanne Prater
Dietitians: Patricia D. Godfrey, R.D., Karen Rubin
Senior Art Director: Sue Schultz
Art Director: Lynn Dolan
Project Manager: Mary O'Brien
Production Consultant: Christine Watkins
Production Manager: Jim Bindas
Assistant Production Manager: Julie Churchill
Typesetting: Jennie Smith, Bryan Trandem
Production Staff: Michelle Alexander, Yelena Konrardy, Nancy Nardone, Nik Wogstad
Photographers: Tony Kubat, Buck Holzemer, Jerry Robb, Kris Boom, Jerry Krause
Food Stylists: Susan Zechmann, Suzanne Finley, Lynn Lohmann, Susan Sinon, Lynne Bachmann
Home Economists: Jill Crum, Peggy Ramette, Kathy Weber
Recipe Editor: Myrna Shaw
Printed in Hong Kong (0195)

CY DECOSSE INCORPORATED
Chairman: Cy DeCosse
President: James B. Maus
Executive Vice President: William B. Jones

Library of Congress Cataloging-in-Publication Data.

Microwaving Light & Healthy

(Microwave cooking library)
Includes index. 1. Microwave Cookery. I. Title. II. Series.
TX832.M3976 1989 641.5'63 85-33484
ISBN 0-86573-564-6

Additional volumes in the Microwave Cooking Library series are available from the publisher:

Contents

What You Need to Know Before You Start

Health and fitness are a personal affair. To maintain them, you need to combine sound nutrition and adequate exercise, but your needs for food and exercise depend on your body and your activity. People with chronic conditions, like high blood pressure or diabetes, should consult a dietitian. Others can improve their nutrition by following the USDA Dietary Guidelines on which the recipes in this book are based.

To stay healthy and fit, you need to maintain your ideal weight. For many of us, that means first dieting to achieve it. The guidelines to sound nutrition can also be guides to sensible dieting. Reasonable reduction in calories combined with exercise can lead to gradual, steady weight loss. The important thing is to learn new eating habits which will keep you healthy. The recipes in this book are designed for normal, sound nutrition. They may help you lose weight gradually, but they are not diet recipes.

Special Ingredients Used in This Book

To reduce calories and sodium even further, the recipes in this book were developed using special ingredients, available nationwide. If you choose not to use these products, you can substitute regular ingredients, recognizing that the calorie, fat, cholesterol and sodium content will be increased. Skim milk, reduced-calorie margarine, butter-flavored mix, low-sodium bouillon granules, "no salt added" vegetables and soups, and other ingredients reduce calorie and sodium content.

Microwave for Natural Goodness

Choosing a nutritious diet is only the beginning. Preparation is important, too. Microwave cooking contributes to healthy eating in three ways.

Microwaving Retains Nutrients

Heat-sensitive or water-soluble nutrients can be lost through prolonged cooking, or drained away with the cooking water. Nutritionists advise brief cooking in a minimum of water for many foods. Microwaving cooks these foods rapidly with little or no added moisture.

Microwaved Food Tastes Good

Microwaving brings out flavors. The natural taste of good food comes through, so salt can be reduced or eliminated. The texture and appearance of microwaved foods enhances their appetite appeal.

Microwaving is Low-Fat

No added fat is needed for microwave cooking, which is non-stick without special pans or additives. Your daily fat allowance can be saved for flavoring food.

Microwaved corn cooks in its own natural moisture for enhanced flavor and nutrition as well as cooking ease.

Three Basics of Healthy Eating

Every day your body needs about forty different nutrients, which work in combination with each other. For example, you need vitamins D and C to utilize calcium. Most foods contain several nutrients, but no single food provides everything you need in the amounts you need. That is one reason why fad diets do not work and can be dangerous. On a single-food diet you risk getting an excess of some nutrients at the expense of others.

1. Variety.

The best way to get all the nutrients you need is to eat a variety of foods. Your daily menu should include vegetables, fruit, whole grain breads or cereals, milk products, meat, poultry or fish, and dried peas or beans. In this way, you will not develop a deficiency of any nutrient, and your meals will be interesting. A monotonous diet, however nutritious, fails because people get bored.

2. Balance.

You not only need a variety of nutrients, you need them in the right proportion. The typical American diet is too high is protein and fat, and skimpy in complex carbohydrates.

3. Moderation.

The portion sizes in this book are based on the USDA recommendations for adults. If you are used to heavier meals, you may feel hungry at first. Adjust your eating habits gradually by supplementing meals with plenty of low-calorie, high-fiber raw vegetables.

Unless you are on a restricted diet prescribed by your physician, lowering fats, sodium and sweeteners need not mean giving them up completely. You can have an occasional pickle or dish of ice cream. If you have a salty or fatty food at one meal, eat salt-free or lean foods at the other two meals.

Eating for health, not dieting, offers a permanent solution to weight problems. The weight you take off gradually will stay off. Following the Dietary Goals may seem like a diet at first. Lowering fats and sweeteners will generally reduce calories automatically. You can make changes in steps; for example, switch from whole milk to 2% for a while, the 2% to 1%, then make the change to skim milk.

Exercise is essential to fitness. A gradual increase in physical activity is safe and will help burn more calories.

Basics of Healthy Eating

Variety of foods provides balanced nutrition and interesting meals.

Reduce fat consumption by changing gradually from whole milk to skim.

Eat plenty of high fiber salad greens, spinach, alfalfa sprouts, mushrooms, zucchini and radishes.

Balanced diet is composed of 10 to 15% protein from animal and vegetable sources, 60% carbohydrates and no more than 25 to 30% fat calories, including the fat content of meats, whole milk, eggs, or cheese.

15% Protein

25% Fat

60% Carbohydrates

What Your Body Needs & How to Get It

Studies show that many Americans suffer from both malnutrition and obesity. They eat more than enough of the wrong kinds of foods.

Protein

Every body needs protein to build tissue and fight infection, but most Americans eat twice as much as they need. Since your body does not store protein, even from meal to meal, you make the best use of it by eating small amounts several times a day. Excess protein is stored in the body as fat. For a 150-pound adult, a 2-ounce serving of meat, fish or chicken provides about one third the daily requirement.

Choose complete or complementary proteins. Most animal proteins: meat, fish, poultry, eggs and milk products, supply all nine of the essential amino acids, and are called complete proteins. Vegetable proteins: dried beans and peas, grains and nuts or seeds, are called incomplete because by themselves they do not supply all the essential amino acids. By eating two or more vegetable proteins together in the proper combinations, called complementary proteins, you can create a complete protein. A small amount of animal protein is enough to supplement a large amount of vegetable protein. Many of the world's traditional dishes are based on complementary combinations. In a balanced diet, one third of your protein should be supplied by animal proteins, and two thirds by complementary vegetable proteins.

Watch out for fatty proteins. Red meats and hard cheeses are high in fat; many contain more fat than protein, and this fat is high in cholesterol and saturated fats.

Low-fat proteins include fish, poultry, veal, lean red meat, low-fat yogurt and dried beans or peas.

Three Ways to Get Complete Protein

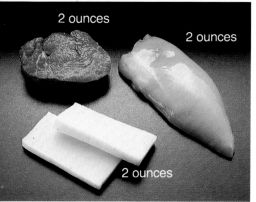

2 ounces

2 ounces

2 ounces

Animal protein is complete protein. Two ounces of steak, chicken or cheese are an adequate serving.

Two or three vegetable proteins, such as corn tortillas or rice with beans, complement each other.

Combinations of vegetable and animal proteins, such as whole wheat spaghetti with a meat ball, make a satisfying meal.

Carbohydrates

Most carbohydrates are not fattening. In fact, a nutritious diet should be about 60% starchy and fibrous carbohydrates. The only carbohydrates you need to avoid are the "empty calorie" sweeteners — sugars, honey and syrups, which are high in calories and almost devoid of nutrients. Complex carbohydrates include beans, peas, nuts, seeds, whole grains and cereals, vegetables and fruits, and are a primary source of vitamins and minerals.

Fiber is supplied by fruits, vegetables and whole grains. Fiber, which our grandparents called "roughage" or "bulk," can help you lose weight by satisfying hunger with fewer calories. It is also a natural laxative. Fiber itself has no nutritional value, but fibrous foods are also rich in nutrients. The best way to get enough fiber in your diet is to eat plenty of these fibrous foods, rather than use pills or food additives.

Starchy foods, like potatoes, dried beans and peas, rice and whole grain breads, cereals and pastas are especially nutritious. It is not the starches which are fattening, it is the butter, cream, gravy or jelly we put on them.

Vitamins & Minerals

Vitamins and minerals are essential nutrients. If you eat a balanced diet, you should get everything you need. Except when prescribed by a qualified professional, vitamin and mineral supplements are needed primarily by people who are on fad diets, who live on snack foods, or by those who either will not eat their vegetables or overcook them. In fact, large doses of several vitamins and minerals can be harmful.

Calcium may be your body's most essential mineral, yet the typical American diet is deficient in calcium. We all know that children need calcium to build bones; adults, especially older adults, need calcium to prevent bone loss, such as peridontal disease and osteoporosis.

Calcium-rich foods are milk products, spinach, collard and mustard greens, kale, broccoli, canned salmon or sardines with bones, and oysters.

What You Should Limit

How much is too much depends on your body and state of health. Almost everyone can benefit from a reduction of fats, cholesterol, sodium and sugars.

Fats & Cholesterol

We all need a little fat in our diet; most of us consume far too much of it. Even if you aim at a low-fat diet, you will get some. "Low fat" is not "no fat."

Cholesterol is found in animal products, including low-calorie organ meats and shrimp. Unless you're on a restricted diet, liver can be eaten occasionally be-cause it is a rich source of iron and vitamins.

Saturated fats, which include the fats in meat, poultry, fish, cheese, lard, butter, egg yolks and solid vegetable shortening, increase the level of cholesterol in the blood.

Unsaturated fats will not in-crease your cholesterol level, but they are just as high in calo-ries as other fats. Most vegetable oils are unsaturated, except for coconut, palm and palm kernel. When vegetable oils are hydro-genated or hardened, they be-come saturated.

Saturated fats and cholesterol in animal products elevate blood cholesterol levels.

How to Select Fats

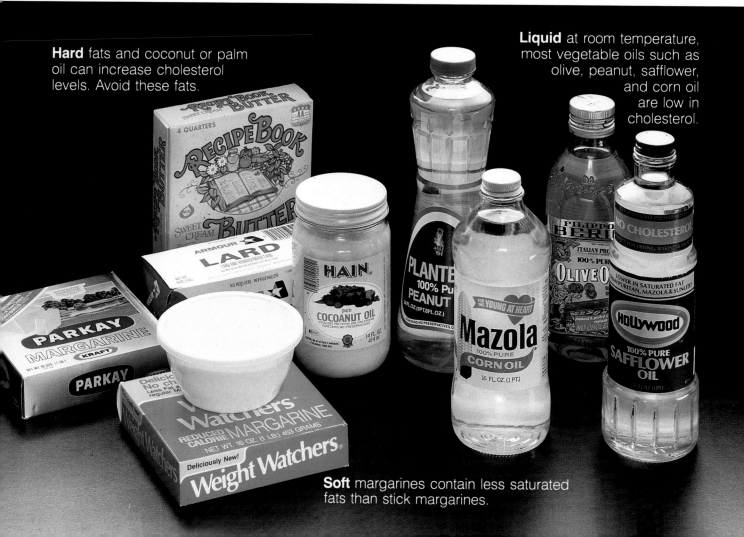

Hard fats and coconut or palm oil can increase cholesterol levels. Avoid these fats.

Liquid at room temperature, most vegetable oils such as olive, peanut, safflower, and corn oil are low in cholesterol.

Soft margarines contain less saturated fats than stick margarines.

Sugar

Sugars are America's leading food additive. They include white and brown sugar, raw sugar, honey, and maple or corn syrups. They can account for almost one fourth of our daily calories without contributing any significant nutrition.

Empty calories can make you overweight. Sticky sweets, especially between-meal snacks, promote tooth decay. For some people sugars are "trigger foods" which can set off binge eating. They start with just one cookie and eat the whole batch.

Avoiding excess sugar does not mean giving up sweets completely. We can stop adding sugar to coffee, tea or cereals. We need to break the habit of eating sweets every day, or worse, with every meal. We can still have an occasional treat.

The dessert section of this book includes recipes for those occasions. Honey and maple syrup are not more natural or better for you than other sugars. They do offer a distinctive flavor which can compensate for reduced sweetness in home-made treats.

Non-sweet foods contain sugar, too. Check the ingredients listing on catsup, crackers, cereal, salad dressing, spaghetti sauce or peanut butter. Some products list honey or corn syrup and sugar. They all add up to sugar. If the first ingredient ends in "ose," such as suc*rose* or fruct*ose*, it contains more sugar than anything else.

How to Reduce Sugar in Your Diet

Serve fresh or juice-packed fruit for dessert. It provides vitamins, minerals and fiber as well as sweetness.

Plan an occasional home-made dessert now and then, rather than indulge in impulse eating. (Cheater's Cheesecake, p. 139)

Avoid sweet snacks, candy and soft drinks between meals.

11

Sodium

Sodium is another element that Americans consume in excess. A high-sodium diet is linked to high blood pressure, kidney disease and edema: bloating or swelling from water retained in the tissues.

Salt used in cooking or added at the table is not the only source of sodium; it is also found in baking powder and soda, and food additives. Some sodium is naturally present in drinking water, dairy products, meats, and some vegetables. More is added in commercial preparation. Products which boast "no preservatives added" may contain salt as a preservative.

Hidden sodium is hard to detect; the foods do not necessarily taste salty. We expect sodium in pickles, sauerkraut, bacon and snack foods, but an ounce of breakfast cereal may contain more sodium than an ounce of potato chips.

Reduce salt in stages. If you omit salt all at once, your food may seem tasteless for a few days. Select fresh or frozen vegetables and microwave them without salt. Taste at the table and salt very lightly if necessary. As you adjust to less salt, reduce the amount added.

Rewards of a low-sodium diet are more than the benefit to your health. After a week or so without added salt, your sense of taste improves. You can actually taste and enjoy the natural flavors of foods.

Canned vegetables, baked goods, cheeses and condiments are also high in sodium. Read food labels carefully and choose low-sodium products.

1 tsp.

Safe daily sodium allowance from all sources is 2000 to 3000 mg, or about 1 teaspoon. One teaspoon of salt contains 2132 mg. of sodium.

Rinse and drain canned vegetables if salt-free products are not available. Some recipes in this book call for a small amount of salt. Omit it if you are cooking for a restricted diet.

Pasta & Grains

◂ Hot Pasta Salad

1 medium green pepper, cut into ¼-inch strips
½ medium red onion, cut in half lengthwise and thinly sliced
2 tablespoons reconstituted natural butter-flavored mix
2 teaspoons poppy seed
⅛ teaspoon salt*
¾ cup cooked spaghetti
1 medium tomato, cut into thin wedges

4 servings

In 1-quart casserole, combine all ingredients, except spaghetti and tomato. Cover. Microwave at High for 3 to 5 minutes, or just until pepper and onion are tender, stirring once. Add remaining ingredients. Toss lightly. Re-cover. Microwave at High for 2 to 3 minutes longer, or until hot. Let stand, covered, for 1 minute.

*To reduce sodium omit salt.

Per Serving:	
Calories:	65
Protein:	2 g.
Carbohydrate:	14 g.
Fat:	—
Cholesterol:	—
Sodium:	—
Calcium:	115 mg.
Exchanges:	½ starch, 1 vegetable

Garlic Rice & Pasta

2 tablespoons reduced-calorie margarine
1 cup uncooked brown rice
½ cup uncooked broken spaghetti
3 cups hot water
2 tablespoons sliced green onion
1 clove garlic, minced
½ teaspoon salt*
⅛ teaspoon pepper
2 tablespoons snipped fresh parsley

8 servings

In 3-quart casserole, combine margarine, rice and spaghetti. Microwave at High for 4 to 7 minutes, or until spaghetti is golden brown, stirring after first 2 minutes, then after every minute. Stir in remaining ingredients, except parsley. Cover. Microwave at High for 5 minutes. Reduce power to 50% (Medium). Microwave for 40 minutes long____ is absorbed a____ ___d parsley. ____tes.

Per S____	
Calories:	
Prot____	
Carb____	
Fat:	
Cholesterol:	
Sodium:	
Calcium:	
Exchanges:	

Rice Me____

½ cup u____
¼ cup u____ rinse____
¼ cup ch____ pepp____
2 tables____ parsle____
1 tables____ celery
2¼ cups ho____
2 tables____
1 teaspoo____ beef b____
¼ teaspoo____
¼ teaspoo____ season____
1 bay leaf

In 2-quart ca____
all ingredient____
Microwave at____

How to Use This Book

This is not a diet book. The recipes are designed for a lifetime of nutritious eating. Fats, cholesterol, sugars and sodium have been cut to an acceptable level. If you are on a restricted diet, you may want to cut them even further. The per-serving nutritional information following each recipe will help you select the foods which suit your personal needs.

Calories. The per-serving calorie measurement indicates total calories. The exchanges identify calorie sources.

Protein. The per-serving measurement includes animal and vegetable sources.

Carbohydrate. The per-serving carbohydrate measurement includes both complex carbohydrates and sugars.

Fat. The per-serving fat measurement includes saturated and unsaturated fats.

Cholesterol. Polyunsaturated vegetable oils have been used wherever possible to reduce cholesterol and saturated fat.

Sodium. Low-sodium ingredients have been used wherever possible.

Calcium. The per-serving calcium measurement given for all foods. A double asterisk indicates recipes which use an excellent source of calcium.

Exchanges. The exchange system is recommended by the American Diabetes Association and several weight-control organizations. It indicates the sources and balance of a food's calories. Based on the revised 1986 ADA exchanges.

Menu Planning

Seven food groups provide variety and nutrition. Choose from proteins (meat, poultry, fish, eggs and cheese), milk, breads (including grains, cereals, pasta and legumes), vegetables, fruits, fats (including avocados, bacon, cream, cream cheese and salad dressings), and free foods (salad greens, herbs and low-calorie condiments).

The easiest way to provide balanced nutrition for yourself and your family is to plan for an entire day rather than meal-by-meal. In this way, extra sodium, fat or calories at one meal can be compensated at another. While breakfast need not be as large as lunch or dinner, your meals should be approximately equal in size. Several small meals are better than one or two large ones.

You do not have to be on a diet to use the exchanges as a guide to planning balanced meals. Make sure the daily menu includes foods from each group. When you serve a medium or high-fat meat, cut down on other fats. If you are using a starch as a protein source, be sure to include its complement at the same meal. Serve grains, like rice, pasta or cereal, with legumes or milk. Combine legumes like dried beans with grains or seeds.

Balanced Nutrition at 1,200 Calories

Meat (low fat)	6
Milk	2
Bread or grain	5
Vegetables	2
Fruits	3
Fats	2
Free Foods	unlimited

How many calories an individual needs to maintain ideal weight depends on age, height, frame, sex and activity. The Balanced Nutrition Chart (left) illustrates a balance between food groups with a 1,200 calorie diet. If well planned, this calorie level will meet all of the daily recommended dietary allowances.

The same basic menu can serve an entire family. Those who need more calories can eat additional servings of milk, vegetables, or fruit, and breads. This sample menu (below) for a full day illustrates the way in which a dieter can eat a 1,200 calorie menu while other family members who can use more calories might eat a menu of 2,000 calories.

Sample Menu For One Day *(Recipes can be found in this book)*

Meal	1200 Calorie Minimum Diet	2000 Calorie Diet *(Pictured, left)*
Breakfast	½ cup orange juice Oatmeal with Prunes & Raisins ½ cup skim milk	½ cup orange juice Oatmeal with Prunes & Raisins *1 cup skim milk* *2 slices Whole Grain Nut Bread* *2 teaspoons margarine*
Lunch	Marinated Vegetables Chicken Taco Lettuce-Carrot Sauté Maple Custard	Marinated Vegetables Chicken Taco *Vegetable & Cheese Enchilada* Lettuce-Carrot Sauté Maple Custard
Dinner	1 Vegetable Kebab with Lemon Dressing Salmon Steak & Caper Sauce Stuffed Tomato Minted Fruit Compote	2 Vegetable Kebabs with Lemon Dressing Salmon Steak & Caper Sauce Stuffed Tomato *Slim Twice-baked Potato* Minted Fruit Compote *Whole Wheat Fig Muffin* *1 teaspoon margarine*

Pictured: 2,000 Calorie Menu

Soups & Appetizers

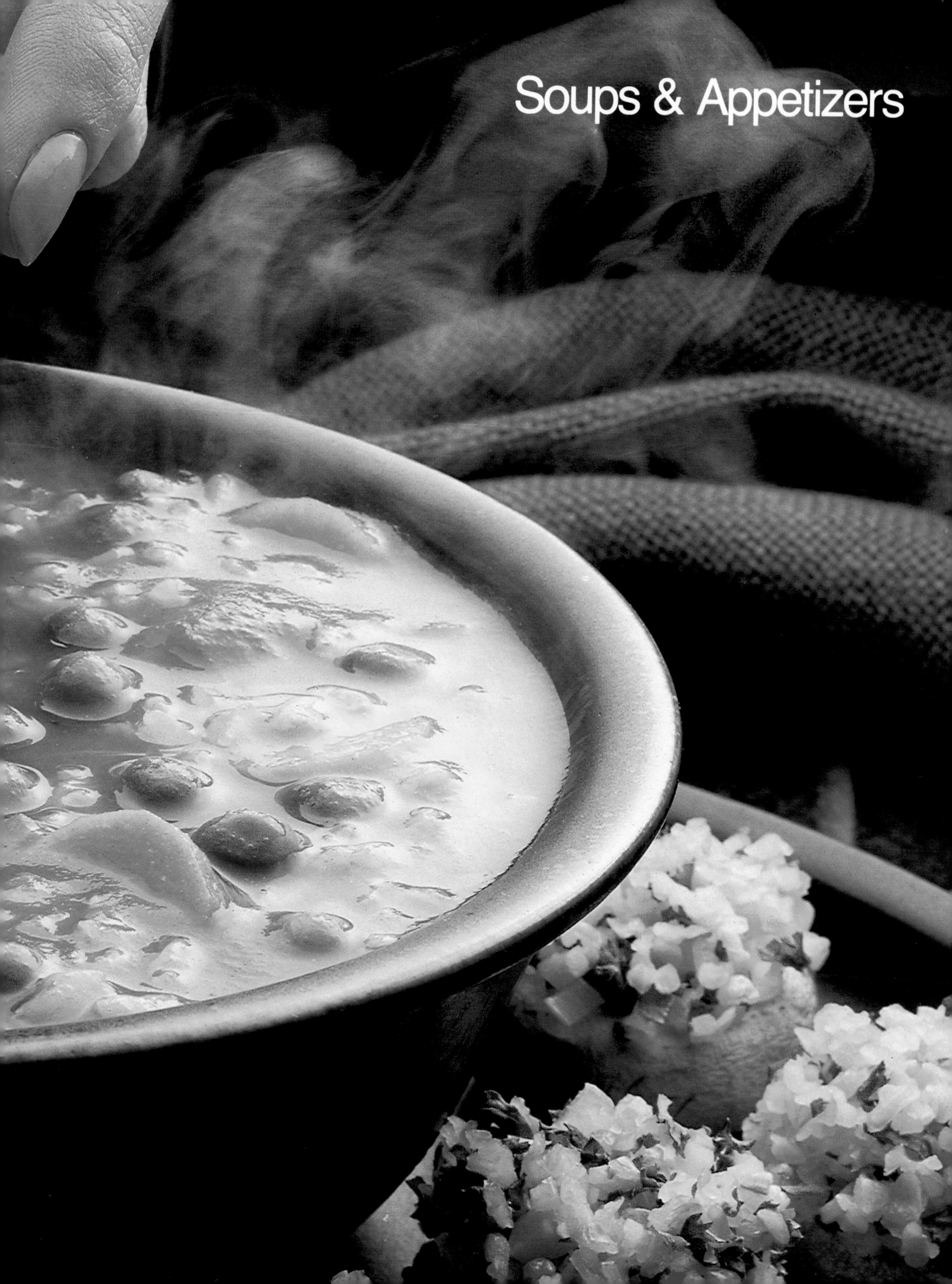

Lentil Onion Soup

1 medium onion, thinly sliced
2 tablespoons reduced-calorie
  margarine
1 clove garlic, minced
⅛ teaspoon pepper
1 cup cooked lentils, page 110
2 cups hot water
2 teaspoons low-sodium instant
  beef bouillon granules
1 tablespoon sherry
1 medium tomato, seeded and
  chopped
2 teaspoons grated Parmesan
  cheese

4 servings, 1 cup each

In 2-quart casserole, combine onion, margarine, garlic and pepper. Cover. Microwave at High for 5 to 6 minutes, or until onion is tender, stirring once. Add remaining ingredients, except cheese. Re-cover. Microwave at High for 7 to 10 minutes, or until tomato is tender. Let stand, covered, for 5 minutes. Sprinkle each serving with Parmesan cheese.

Per Serving:	
Calories:	73
Protein:	5 g.
Carbohydrate:	13 g.
Fat:	—
Cholesterol:	—
Sodium:	34 mg.
Calcium:	30 mg.
Exchanges:	½ starch, 1 vegetable

Cream of Broccoli ▲ & Cauliflower Soup

1 pkg. (10 oz.) frozen chopped broccoli
1 pkg. (10 oz.) frozen cauliflower
1 cup shredded potato
1 cup water
2 tablespoons chopped onion
2 teaspoons low-sodium instant chicken bouillon granules
¼ teaspoon pepper
⅛ teaspoon ground nutmeg
3 cups skim milk

9 servings, ¾ cup each

In 2-quart casserole, combine all ingredients, except milk. Cover. Microwave at High for 15 to 21 minutes, or until vegetables are tender, stirring 2 or 3 times. Let stand, covered, for 5 minutes. Process half the vegetables in food processor or blender bowl until pureed. Repeat with remaining vegetables. Return to casserole. Blend in milk. Microwave, uncovered, at High for 7 to 13 minutes, or until heated through, stirring once or twice.

Per Serving:	
Calories:	59
Protein:	5 g.
Carbohydrate:	10 g.
Fat:	—
Cholesterol:	1 mg.
Sodium:	56 mg.
Calcium:	123 mg.**
Exchanges:	1 vegetable, ½ skim milk

Tomato Rice Soup

1 can (14½ oz.) no-salt stewed tomatoes
1 can (12 oz.) no-salt tomato juice
1 cup hot water
1 cup cooked brown rice, page 111
¼ cup thinly sliced carrot
1 tablespoon frozen orange juice concentrate
1 teaspoon low-sodium instant chicken bouillon granules
⅛ teaspoon pepper
  Dash ground cloves
  Dash ground nutmeg
1 cup frozen peas

10 servings, ½ cup each

In 2-quart casserole, combine all ingredients, except peas. Stir. Cover. Microwave at High for 10 minutes. Add peas. Re-cover. Microwave at High for 5 to 10 minutes longer, or until carrot is tender. Let stand, covered, for 5 minutes.

Per Serving:	
Calories:	55
Protein:	2 g.
Carbohydrate:	12 g.
Fat:	—
Cholesterol:	—
Sodium:	31 mg.
Calcium:	4 mg.
Exchanges:	½ starch, 1 vegetable

Creamy Pumpkin Soup

1 cup hot water
¾ cup canned pumpkin
3 tablespoons thinly sliced green onions
2 teaspoons frozen orange juice concentrate
1½ teaspoons low-sodium instant chicken bouillon granules
¼ teaspoon ground cinnamon
⅛ teaspoon ground ginger
½ cup skim milk

4 servings, ½ cup each

In 1-quart casserole, combine all ingredients, except milk. Mix well. Cover. Microwave at High for 3½ to 5½ minutes, or until bubbly and onions are just tender-crisp, stirring once. Stir in milk. Microwave at High for 30 seconds to 1 minute longer, or until hot. Stir before serving.

Per Serving:	
Calories:	36
Protein:	2 g.
Carbohydrate:	7 g.
Fat:	—
Cholesterol:	—
Sodium:	20 mg.
Calcium:	53 mg.
Exchanges:	½ starch

◄ Oriental Soup

1 cup (½-inch cubes) turnips
½ cup julienne carrots
   (2 × ⅛-inch strips)
1 clove garlic, minced
2 cups shredded lettuce
1 cup bean sprouts
1 pkg. (6 oz.) frozen pea pods
3 cups hot water
2 tablespoons reduced-sodium
   soy sauce
1 tablespoon low-sodium
   instant chicken bouillon
   granules
¼ teaspoon sesame oil
⅛ teaspoon white pepper
⅛ teaspoon ground ginger

     5 servings, 1 cup each

In 2-quart casserole, combine
turnips, carrots and garlic.
Cover. Microwave at High for 6
to 7 minutes, or until tender.
Add remaining ingredients.
Re-cover. Microwave at High for
10 to 15 minutes longer, or until
hot and lettuce is wilted, stirring
after half the time to break apart
pea pods.

Per Serving:	
Calories:	46
Protein:	2 g.
Carbohydrate:	9 g.
Fat:	—
Cholesterol:	—
Sodium:	154 mg.
Calcium:	34 mg.
Exchanges:	2 vegetable

Split Pea & Ham Soup ▲

1 lb. dried green split peas,
   sorted, rinsed and drained
6 cups hot water
1 cup (¼-inch cubes) potato
½ cup thinly sliced carrot
⅓ cup chopped low-fat boiled
   ham (about 2 oz.)
2 teaspoons low-sodium
   instant chicken bouillon
   granules
1 teaspoon dried thyme leaves
1 bay leaf
24 whole peppercorns

     10 servings, ¾ cup each

In 5-quart casserole, combine
all ingredients. Stir. Cover.
Microwave at High for 10
minutes. Reduce power to 50%
(Medium). Microwave for 30
minutes. Stir and re-cover.
Microwave at 50% (Medium) for
30 to 45 minutes longer, or until
peas are tender. Let stand,
covered, for 10 to 15 minutes.
Remove bay leaf and
peppercorns before serving.

Per Serving:	
Calories:	83
Protein:	5 g.
Carbohydrate:	13 g.
Fat:	2 g.
Cholesterol:	3 mg.
Sodium:	93 mg.
Calcium:	25 mg.
Exchanges:	1 starch

Tomato Cucumber Aspic

1 envelope unflavored gelatin
½ cup cold water
1 can (12 oz.) no-salt tomato
   juice
1 tablespoon frozen apple juice
   concentrate
½ teaspoon low-sodium instant
   beef bouillon granules
⅛ teaspoon pepper
1 bay leaf
1 cup peeled, seeded and
   chopped cucumber
2 tablespoons sliced green
   onion

5 servings, ½ cup each

Per Serving:	
Calories:	28
Protein:	2 g.
Carbohydrate:	6 g.
Fat:	—
Cholesterol:	—
Sodium:	10 mg.
Calcium:	—
Exchanges:	1 vegetable

How to Microwave Tomato Cucumber Aspic

Soften gelatin in cold water in 1-cup measure. Set aside. In 4-cup measure, combine tomato juice, apple juice concentrate, bouillon, pepper and bay leaf.

Microwave at High for 2½ to 5 minutes, or until boiling. Remove bay leaf.

Add softened gelatin mixture. Stir until gelatin dissolves. Chill until thickened but not set (about 2 hours).

Fold in cucumber and onion. Spray 3 to 4-cup mold with vegetable cooking spray.

Pour into prepared mold. Chill until set (about 2 hours).

Dip mold into warm water for 30 seconds. Loosen edges and unmold onto serving plate.

Vegetable Kebabs with Lemon Dressing

Lemon Dressing:

3 tablespoons reconstituted
    natural butter-flavored mix
1 tablespoon lemon juice
¼ teaspoon onion powder
⅛ teaspoon dried marjoram
    leaves
    Dash pepper

8 frozen whole Brussels sprouts
    (about 1 cup)
8 frozen whole baby carrots
    (about ¾ cup)
8 fresh cauliflowerets, 1-inch
    pieces (about 1 cup)
1 small green pepper, cut into
    16 chunks
8 wooden skewers, 6-inch
2 tablespoons water

      8 servings, 1 kebab each

In 1-cup measure, blend all dressing ingredients. Set aside. In 1-quart casserole, combine frozen Brussels sprouts and carrots. Cover. Microwave at High for 1½ to 3 minutes, or until defrosted. Let stand, covered, for 5 minutes.

For each kebab, assemble one Brussels sprout, carrot, green pepper chunk, caulifloweret and another green pepper chunk on wooden skewer. Repeat to make 8 kebabs. Arrange on platter with Brussels sprouts toward center. Sprinkle with water. Cover with plastic wrap. Microwave at High for 3 to 5 minutes, or until tender-crisp, rotating platter once. Let stand, covered, for 3 to 4 minutes. Pour dressing over kebabs. Serve hot.

Per Serving:	
Calories:	21
Protein:	1 g.
Carbohydrate:	5 g.
Fat:	—
Cholesterol:	—
Sodium:	49 mg.
Calcium:	12 mg.
Exchanges:	1 vegetable

Stuffed Mushrooms

½ cup water
2 tablespoons bulgur or
   cracked wheat
8 oz. whole fresh mushrooms
   (reserve stems)
2 tablespoons snipped fresh
   parsley
1 tablespoon finely chopped
   onion
1 teaspoon lemon juice
⅛ teaspoon fennel seed
   Dash ground sage
   Dash pepper
2 tablespoons grated
   Parmesan cheese

6 servings

Place water in 1-cup measure. Microwave at High for 1½ to 2½ minutes, or until water boils. Place bulgur in small bowl. Add boiling water. Cover and let stand 1 hour to soften. Drain and press out excess moisture. Set aside. Remove stems from mushrooms. Set mushroom caps aside. Chop enough stems to equal 2 tablespoons. In 1-quart casserole, combine mushroom stems, parsley, onion, lemon juice, fennel, sage and pepper. Microwave at High for 1 to 2 minutes, or until tender. Stir in bulgur and cheese. Fill mushroom caps with mixture, mounding slightly. Arrange caps filled-side-up on plate. Microwave at High for 2½ to 4½ minutes, or until tender, rotating plate once. Let stand for 3 to 5 minutes. Serve hot.

Per Serving:
Calories:	29
Protein:	7 g.
Carbohydrate:	4 g.
Fat:	1 g.
Cholesterol:	1 mg.
Sodium:	32 mg.
Calcium:	27 mg.
Exchanges:	1 vegetable

Lentil Pâté ▲

2 tablespoons snipped fresh
   parsley
1 tablespoon minced onion
1 clove garlic, minced
3 tablespoons reduced-calorie
   margarine
½ teaspoon low-sodium instant
   chicken bouillon granules

1 can (16 oz.) pinto beans,
   rinsed and drained
1 cup cooked lentils, page 110
¼ teaspoon pepper
1 tablespoon sherry

26 servings, 1 tablespoon each

In small mixing bowl, combine parsley, onion, garlic, margarine and bouillon. Cover. Microwave at High for 1 to 2 minutes, or until margarine melts. Pour into food processor bowl. Add remaining ingredients. Process until smooth. Spoon mixture into small crock. Cover and chill until firm. Serve as a spread with unsalted crackers.

Per Serving:
Calories:	30	Cholesterol:	—
Protein:	1 g.	Sodium:	34 mg.
Carbohydrate:	4 g.	Calcium:	2 mg.
Fat:	2 g.	Exchanges:	1 vegetable

Marinated Vegetables

6 cherry tomatoes, cut in half
1 small onion, thinly sliced
1 pkg. (10 oz.) frozen cut
    green beans
1 pkg. (9 oz.) frozen
    artichoke hearts
2 cups fresh broccoli flowerets
1 medium yellow or zucchini
    squash, quartered
    lengthwise and cut into
    1½-inch pieces
½ cup thinly sliced carrot

Dressing:

½ cup red wine vinegar
2 tablespoons vegetable oil
1 clove garlic, minced
½ teaspoon bouquet garni
    seasoning
¼ teaspoon pepper

12 servings, ½ cup each

In large mixing bowl, combine
tomatoes and onion. Set aside.
Unwrap beans and place on
plate. Microwave at High for 3
to 4 minutes, or until defrosted.
Let stand for 5 minutes. Repeat
for artichoke hearts.

In 1½-quart casserole, combine
broccoli, squash and carrot.
Cover. Microwave at High for
3 to 6 minutes, or until broccoli
is bright green and carrots are
tender-crisp. Add beans,
artichoke hearts, broccoli,
squash and carrot to tomatoes
and onion. Stir to combine.

In 2-cup measure, combine all
dressing ingredients. Microwave
at High for 30 seconds to 1½
minutes, or until warm. Pour
over vegetables. Toss to coat.
Cover and chill at least 4 hours
before serving.

Per Serving:
Calories: 29
Protein: 2 g.
Carbohydrate: 7 g.
Fat: —
Cholesterol: —
Sodium: 10 mg.
Calcium: 46 mg.
Exchanges: 1 vegetable

Turkey-on-a-Stick

¼ cup sliced green onions
¼ cup shredded carrot
1 clove garlic, minced
1 lb. ground turkey
2 egg whites
⅓ cup rolled oats
2 tablespoons no-salt ketchup
½ teaspoon chili powder
¼ teaspoon dry mustard
¼ teaspoon paprika
¼ teaspoon liquid smoke
⅛ teaspoon cayenne

10 wooden skewers, 6-inch

Coating:

¼ cup cornflake crumbs
⅛ teaspoon paprika
    Dash cayenne

Tangy Mustard Sauce:

¼ cup Tangy Topper, page 27
1 tablespoon prepared
    mustard
1 teaspoon snipped fresh
    parsley

10 servings

Per Serving:			
Calories:	115	Cholesterol:	41 mg.
Protein:	16 g.	Sodium:	197 mg.
Carbohydrate:	7 g.	Calcium:	24 mg.
Fat:	3 g.	Exchanges:	2 lean meat, 1 vegetable

How to Microwave Turkey-on-a-Stick

Mix together onions, carrot and garlic in 1-quart casserole. Cover. Microwave at High for 1½ to 2½ minutes, or until tender-crisp.

Combine remaining ingredients, except coating and Tangy Mustard Sauce, in medium mixing bowl. Mix well.

Divide turkey mixture into 10 equal portions, using ¼ cup for each. Shape into about 3-inch oval loaves. Insert wooden skewer into each loaf.

Blend all coating ingredients on wax paper. Roll each loaf in coating. Arrange on roasting rack, skewers toward center.

Microwave at High for 6 to 9 minutes, or until turkey is firm to touch and cooked through, rotating rack once.

Let turkey stand for 3 to 4 minutes. In small bowl, blend all Tangy Mustard Sauce ingredients. Serve turkey with sauce.

◀ Chunky Salsa Sauce

1 cup chopped onion
1 clove garlic, minced
1 can (14½ oz.) no-salt whole
　tomatoes, cut-up
1 can (8 oz.) no-salt tomato
　sauce
1 can (4 oz.) diced green
　chilies, rinsed and drained
1 teaspoon ground cumin
½ teaspoon dried oregano
　leaves
¼ teaspoon dried crushed
　red pepper

26 servings, 2 tablespoons each

In 2-quart casserole, combine
onion and garlic. Cover. Microwave at High for 2 to 4 minutes,
or until onion is tender-crisp. Stir
in remaining ingredients. Microwave, uncovered, at High for 8
to 11 minutes, or until hot and
flavors are blended, stirring
once or twice. Chill at least 4
hours before serving. Serve as
a dip or sauce with fresh
vegetables or tacos.

Per Serving:	
Calories:	9
Protein:	—
Carbohydrate:	2 g.
Fat:	—
Cholesterol:	—
Sodium:	4 mg.
Calcium:	2 mg.
Exchanges:	free

Mexican Bean Dip ▲

½ cup chopped onion
⅓ cup chopped green pepper
1 clove garlic, minced
½ teaspoon ground cumin
¼ teaspoon pepper
1 can (15 oz.) garbanzo beans,
　rinsed and drained, or 1½
　cups cooked garbanzo
　beans, page 110
2 tablespoons water
½ cup seeded and chopped
　fresh tomato

26 servings, 1 tablespoon each

In 1-quart casserole, combine
onion, green pepper, garlic,
cumin and pepper. Stir. Cover.
Microwave at High for 2 to 4½
minutes, or until tender, stirring
once. In food processor or
blender bowl, process vegetable mixture, beans and
water until pureed. Return to
casserole. Stir in tomato. Cover.
Microwave at High for 2 to 3
minutes, or until hot, stirring
once. Serve as a dip or spread.

TIP: When using cooked
garbanzo beans, increase water
to 3 tablespoons.

Per Serving:	
Calories:	17
Protein:	1 g.
Carbohydrate:	3 g.
Fat:	—
Cholesterol:	—
Sodium:	55 mg.
Calcium:	—
Exchanges:	½ vegetable

Pita Pizza Snacks ▶

2 whole wheat pita breads,
   4-inch
¼ cup prepared Basic Tomato
   Sauce, page 98, divided
¼ cup shredded low-moisture,
   part-skim mozzarella
   cheese, divided
2 tablespoons chopped green
   pepper, divided
¼ cup sliced mushrooms,
   divided

4 servings

Split pita breads in half. Toast.
Top each half with tomato
sauce, cheese, green pepper
and mushrooms. Place on
paper towel-lined serving plate.
Microwave at 70% (Medium
High) for 1½ to 2 minutes, or
until cheese melts, rotating plate
after half the time.

Per Serving:
Calories:	85
Protein:	6 g.
Carbohydrate:	9 g.
Fat:	3 g.
Cholesterol:	8 mg.
Sodium:	146 mg.
Calcium:	104 mg.**
Exchanges:	½ starch, ½ med.-fat meat, ½ vegetable

Tangy Topper ▶

1 cup low-fat cottage cheese
¼ cup low-fat plain yogurt
½ teaspoon fresh lemon juice

16 servings, 1 tablespoon each

In blender container, combine
all ingredients. Blend until
smooth. Chill thoroughly. Use in
salad dressings or as a topping
in place of sour cream.

Per Serving:
Calories:	13
Protein:	2 g.
Carbohydrate:	1 g.
Fat:	—
Cholesterol:	1 mg.
Sodium:	72 mg.
Calcium:	15 mg.
Exchanges:	free

Main Dishes

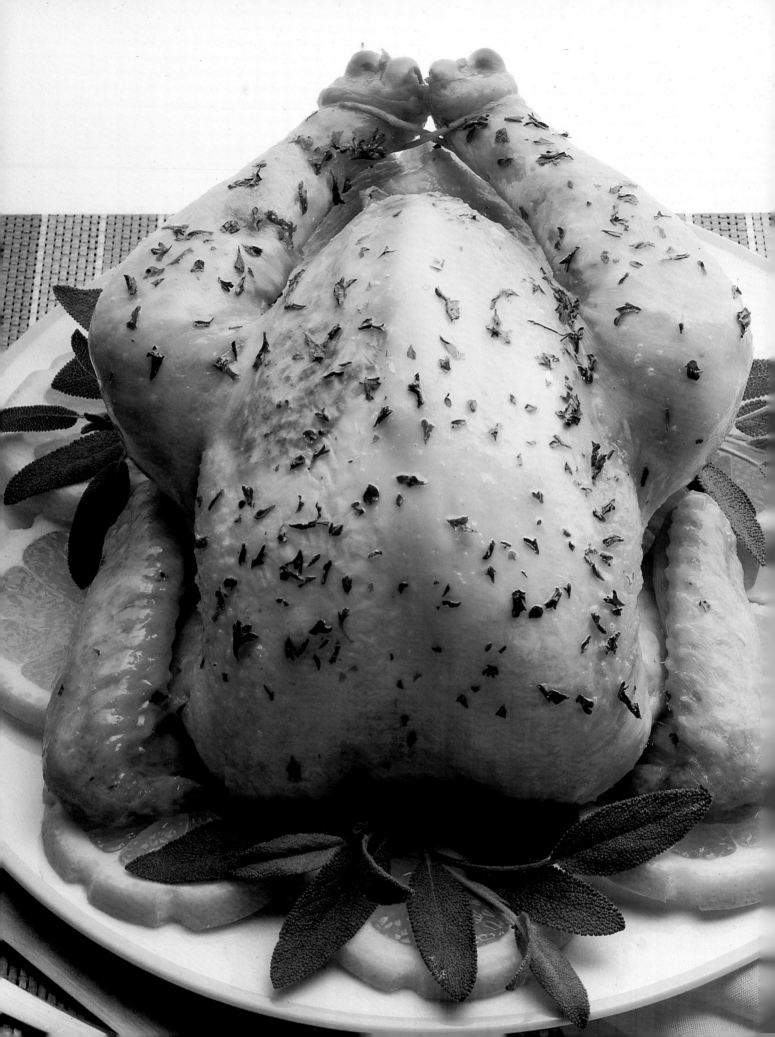

Poultry

◄ Herb-roasted Chicken

½ teaspoon grated lemon peel
½ teaspoon dried oregano
  leaves
¼ teaspoon crushed sage
¼ teaspoon dried marjoram
  leaves
¼ teaspoon pepper, divided
⅛ teaspoon instant minced
  garlic

2½ to 3-lb. whole broiler-fryer
  chicken
1 small onion, sliced
1 bay leaf
½ teaspoon dried parsley
  flakes

4 servings

Per Serving:			
Calories:	178	Cholesterol:	81 mg.
Protein:	26 g.	Sodium:	79 mg.
Carbohydrate:	1 g.	Calcium:	22 mg.
Fat:	7 g.	Exchanges:	3½ lean meat

How to Microwave Herb-roasted Chicken

Mix lemon peel, oregano, sage, marjoram, ⅛ teaspoon pepper and garlic in small bowl.

Gently loosen and lift skin from breast and legs. Rub herb mixture under skin. Replace skin. Place onion and bay leaf in cavity of chicken.

Secure legs together with string. In small bowl, mix parsley and ⅛ teaspoon pepper. Rub onto chicken skin. Place chicken breast-side up on roasting rack.

Microwave at High for 18 to 24 minutes, or until legs move freely and juices run clear, rotating rack twice. Let chicken stand, covered, for 10 minutes before carving.

Cinnamon Orange Spiced Chicken

2 whole bone-in chicken
  breasts (about 12 oz. each)
  split in half, skin removed

Marinade:
¼ cup fresh orange juice
2 tablespoons vermouth
1 teaspoon grated orange peel
1 teaspoon Worcestershire
  sauce
1 teaspoon onion powder
½ teaspoon ground cinnamon
¼ teaspoon ground allspice
  Dash cayenne
1 bay leaf

4 orange slices

4 servings

Place chicken breast halves in large plastic food storage bag or glass dish. Set aside. In 1-cup measure, blend all marinade ingredients except bay leaf. Pour over chicken. Add bay leaf. Secure bag or cover dish. Marinate in refrigerator for at least 4 hours or overnight, turning chicken over once.

Remove chicken from marinade. Arrange on roasting rack with thickest portions toward outside. Cover with wax paper. Microwave at High for 8 to 15 minutes, or until juices run clear and chicken is no longer pink, rotating rack twice. Remove bay leaf. Top with orange slices.

Per Serving:	
Calories:	150
Protein:	27 g.
Carbohydrate:	4 g.
Fat:	2 g.
Cholesterol:	68 mg.
Sodium:	91 mg.
Calcium:	—
Exchanges:	3 lean meat

31

One-Dish Hungarian Dinner

2 cups chopped cabbage
1 cup chopped onion
1 medium green pepper, cut into ½-inch strips
½ cup sliced carrots, ½ inch thick
2 tablespoons water
1 teaspoon paprika
½ teaspoon low-sodium instant chicken bouillon granules
¼ teaspoon caraway seed
¼ teaspoon dried thyme leaves
¼ teaspoon dried dill weed
1 can (16 oz.) Great Northern beans, rinsed and drained
1 can (6 oz.) no-salt tomato paste
2 tablespoons frozen apple juice concentrate
½ cup light beer
2½ to 3-lb. broiler-fryer chicken, cut into 8 pieces, skin removed
Paprika
6 tablespoons Tangy Topper, page 27

6 servings

In 3-quart casserole, combine cabbage, onion, green pepper, carrots, water, paprika, bouillon, caraway, thyme and dill. Cover. Microwave at High for 9 to 12 minutes, or until tender, stirring once. Stir in beans, tomato paste, apple juice and beer. Arrange chicken on vegetable mixture. Cover. Reduce power to 70% (Medium High). Microwave for 25 to 29 minutes, or until chicken near bone is no longer pink, rearranging chicken after every 10 minutes. Let stand, covered, for 5 minutes. Sprinkle chicken with paprika before serving. Top each serving with 1 tablespoon Tangy Topper.

Per Serving:
Calories:	226
Protein:	25 g.
Carbohydrate:	27 g.
Fat:	5 g.
Cholesterol:	57 mg.
Sodium:	206 mg.
Calcium:	49 mg.
Exchanges:	1 starch, 2 lean meat, 2 vegetable

Chicken Coatings

Bran Herb Coating:

1½ cups bran flake cereal,
    finely crushed in blender
⅓ cup cornflake crumbs
2 tablespoons grated
    Parmesan cheese
½ teaspoon ground marjoram
¼ teaspoon dried rosemary
    leaves, crushed
¼ teaspoon pepper

**Spicy Poppy Seed Crumb
Coating:**

⅔ cup fine unseasoned dry
    bread crumbs
3 tablespoons wheat germ
2 teaspoons poppy seed
½ teaspoon onion powder
¼ teaspoon garlic powder
¼ teaspoon dry mustard
¼ teaspoon paprika
¼ teaspoon cayenne

2 tablespoons reduced-calorie
    margarine
2 egg whites
2½ to 3-lb. broiler-fryer chicken,
    cut into 8 pieces, skin
    removed

4 servings

In shallow bowl, combine all coating ingredients for either recipe. Set aside. Place margarine in shallow bowl. Microwave at 70% (Medium High) for 20 to 30 seconds, or just until margarine melts. Beat egg whites into margarine with fork. Dip chicken in egg mixture, then roll in crumb mixture, pressing lightly to coat. Arrange chicken on roasting rack, bone-side down.

Microwave at High for 8 minutes. Rearrange chicken. Do not turn chicken over. Microwave for 5 to 11 minutes longer, or until chicken near bone is no longer pink and juices run clear. Let stand for 3 minutes.

Per Serving:	
Calories:	260
Protein:	31 g.
Carbohydrate:	14 g.
Fat:	13 g.
Cholesterol:	85 mg.
Sodium:	330 mg.
Calcium:	—
Exchanges:	1 starch, 3½ lean meat

Coriander Chicken with Sweet & Sour Sauce

2 boneless whole chicken
    breasts (about 12 oz. each)
    skin removed, split in half

Herb Filling:

1 tablespoon finely chopped
    green onion
1 teaspoon dried parsley flakes
¼ teaspoon ground coriander
⅛ teaspoon garlic powder
⅛ teaspoon pepper

1 can (8 oz.) unsweetened
    pineapple chunks, drained
    (reserve juice)
¼ cup water
2 tablespoons low-sugar
    orange marmalade
1 tablespoon cornstarch
1 tablespoon no-salt ketchup
2 teaspoons reduced-sodium
    soy sauce
1½ teaspoons white wine vinegar
½ teaspoon low-sodium instant
    chicken bouillon granules
½ cup halved seedless green
    grapes

4 servings

Per Serving:	
Calories:	203
Protein:	27 g.
Carbohydrate:	19 g.
Fat:	2 g.
Cholesterol:	68 mg.
Sodium:	173 mg.
Calcium:	—
Exchanges:	3 lean meat, 1 fruit

How to Microwave Coriander Chicken with Sweet & Sour Sauce

Pound each chicken breast half
to ¼-inch thickness. Set aside.
In small bowl, combine all filling
ingredients. Mix well.

Spread about 1 teaspoonful
filling over each chicken breast
half. Fold in sides and roll up,
enclosing filling.

Place breast seam-side down in
9-inch square baking dish. Add
pineapple chunks to chicken.
Set aside.

Combine remaining ingredients, except grapes, with pineapple juice in 2-cup measure. Mix well.

Microwave at High for 3 to 4 minutes, or until mixture thickens, stirring after every minute. Pour over chicken. Cover with wax paper.

Microwave at High for 6 to 10 minutes, or until chicken is no longer pink, rotating dish once. Sprinkle grapes over chicken during last 2 minutes.

Moroccan Chicken Stew

1 cup sliced carrots, ¼ inch
   thick
1 medium onion, cut into
   ½-inch pieces
1 cup (¼-inch cubes) rutabaga
½ teaspoon ground coriander
¼ teaspoon ground cinnamon
¼ teaspoon cayenne
¼ teaspoon caraway seed
⅛ teaspoon pepper
1 medium zucchini, cut into
   ¼-inch slices
1 can (14½ oz.) no-salt whole
   tomatoes
¼ cup raisins
½ teaspoon salt*
1 pkg. (12 oz.) frozen cooked
   squash
2 whole bone-in chicken
   breasts (about 12 oz. each)
   split in half, skin removed

                      4 servings

In 3-quart casserole, combine
carrots, onion, rutabaga,
coriander, cinnamon, cayenne,
caraway and pepper. Cover.
Microwave at High for 9 to 13
minutes, or until vegetables are
tender, stirring twice. Stir in
zucchini, tomatoes, raisins and
salt. Set aside.

Unwrap squash and place on
plate. Microwave at High for 4
minutes, or until defrosted. Add
to vegetable mixture. Arrange
chicken breast halves on
vegetable mixture. Cover.
Microwave at High for 20 to 25
minutes, or until chicken near
bone is no longer pink, turning
chicken over and rearranging
after half the time. Serve
chicken with vegetable mixture
on couscous, if desired.

*To reduce sodium omit salt.

Per Serving:	
Calories:	233
Protein:	29 g.
Carbohydrate:	25 g.
Fat:	2 g.
Cholesterol:	68 mg.
Sodium:	346 mg.
Calcium:	58 mg.
Exchanges:	1 starch, 3 lean meat, 2 vegetable

Chicken-Vegetable Stew

1 pkg. (10 oz.) frozen baby
    lima beans
1 medium onion, thinly sliced
¼ cup thinly sliced celery
¼ cup chopped carrot
2 tablespoons snipped fresh
    parsley
2½ to 3-lb. broiler-fryer chicken,
    cut into 8 pieces, skin
    removed
2 tablespoons plus 1
    teaspoon cornstarch
½ teaspoon lemon-pepper
    seasoning
½ teaspoon poultry seasoning
¼ teaspoon dried rosemary
    leaves
1 can (10½ oz.) ready-to-serve
    low-sodium chicken broth
2 teaspoons lemon juice

6 servings

Unwrap beans and place on plate. Microwave at High for 2 to 3 minutes, or until defrosted. Set aside. In 3-quart casserole, combine onion, celery, carrot and parsley. Cover. Microwave at High for 4 to 5 minutes, or until tender, stirring once. Add lima beans.

Arrange chicken over vegetables. In 2-cup measure, combine cornstarch, lemon-pepper, poultry seasoning and rosemary. Blend in chicken broth and lemon juice. Pour over chicken. Cover. Microwave at 70% (Medium High) for 25 to 33 minutes, or until chicken near bone is no longer pink and juices run clear, rearranging chicken and stirring sauce after every 10 minutes. Let stand, covered, for 5 minutes.

Per Serving:	
Calories:	322
Protein:	35 g.
Carbohydrate:	34 g.
Fat:	5 g.
Cholesterol:	84 mg.
Sodium:	152 mg.
Calcium:	64 mg.
Exchanges:	2 starch, 3 lean meat, 1 vegetable

Savory Stewed Chicken ▲

2½ to 3-lb. broiler-fryer chicken,
    cut into 8 pieces, skin
    removed
1 can (10½ oz.) ready-to-serve
    low-sodium chicken broth
1 medium onion, thinly sliced
½ cup chopped carrot
½ cup sliced fresh mushrooms
⅓ cup white wine

1 tablespoon snipped fresh
    parsley
1 thin slice lemon
1 teaspoon dried summer
    savory leaves
¼ teaspoon dried thyme
    leaves
⅛ teaspoon pepper
2 cloves garlic, cut in half

4 servings

In 3-quart casserole, combine all ingredients. Cover. Microwave at High for 20 to 30 minutes, or until chicken near bone is no longer pink, turning chicken over and rearranging after half the time. Serve in bowls with broth.

Per Serving:			
Calories:	200	Cholesterol:	2 mg.
Protein:	27 g.	Sodium:	117 mg.
Carbohydrate:	7 g.	Calcium:	—
Fat:	5 g.	Exchanges:	3 lean meat, 1½ vegetable

Summer Chicken Salad ▲

3 cups water
1 cup bulgur or cracked wheat
1 boneless whole chicken
    breast (about 12 oz.) skin
    removed
1 cup seeded chopped
    cucumber
¼ cup chopped red onion
1 tablespoon snipped fresh
    parsley
3 tablespoons reconstituted
    natural butter-flavored mix
2 tablespoons pine nuts
1 tablespoon olive oil
1 tablespoon white wine
    vinegar
½ teaspoon dried basil leaves
⅛ teaspoon garlic powder
1 medium tomato, seeded
    and chopped
¼ teaspoon salt*

6 servings

Place water in 4-cup measure. Microwave at High for 5½ to 7 minutes, or until water boils. Place bulgur in medium mixing bowl. Add boiling water. Cover and let stand for 30 minutes. Drain and press out excess moisture. Set aside.

Place chicken breast on roasting rack. Cover with wax paper. Microwave at High for 4 to 5 minutes, or until chicken is no longer pink, turning chicken over after half the time. Set aside to cool.

In 1½-quart casserole, combine cucumber, onion, parsley, butter-flavored mix, pine nuts, olive oil, vinegar, basil and garlic powder. Mix well. Cover. Microwave at High for 3 to 4 minutes, or until cucumber is translucent, stirring after half the time. Cut chicken into ½-inch cubes. Add chicken, tomato and salt to vegetable mixture. Mix well. Chill for at least 2 hours before serving salad.

*To reduce sodium omit salt.

Per Serving:			
Calories:	178	Cholesterol:	23 mg.
Protein:	11 g.	Sodium:	74 mg.
Carbohydrate:	25 g.	Calcium:	—
Fat:	4 g.	Exchanges:	1 starch, 1 lean meat, 2 vegetable

Garlic Chicken with Pasta

7 oz. uncooked linguine
1 boneless whole chicken
    breast (about 12 oz.) skin
    removed, cut into ¾-inch
    cubes
2 cloves garlic, minced
½ cup reconstituted natural
    butter-flavored mix
2 tablespoons snipped fresh
    parsley
¼ cup skim milk
1 tablespoon grated Parmesan
    cheese
⅛ teaspoon paprika

4 servings

Prepare linguine as directed on
package. Rinse with warm
water. Drain and place in large
serving bowl. Set aside.

In 1-quart casserole, combine
chicken and garlic. Cover.
Microwave at High for 3 to 5
minutes, or until chicken is no
longer pink, stirring after every
minute. Drain. Set aside.

In 2-cup measure, combine
butter-flavored mix, parsley and
milk. Microwave at High for 1 to
1½ minutes, or just until mixture
boils. Pour over chicken. Mix
well. Top linguine with chicken
and sauce. Toss to coat.
Combine Parmesan cheese and
paprika. Sprinkle over linguine.

Per Serving:	
Calories:	260
Protein:	21 g.
Carbohydrate:	39 g.
Fat:	2 g.
Cholesterol:	35 mg.
Sodium:	281 mg.
Calcium:	60 mg.
Exchanges:	2½ starch, 2 lean meat

Simmered Chicken with Barley

2½ to 3-lb. whole broiler-fryer
    chicken
    Pepper
1 medium onion, cut into
    quarters
1 can (8 oz.) no-salt tomato
    sauce
1 cup ready-to-serve
    low-sodium chicken broth
½ cup rosé wine
1½ cups sliced fresh
    mushrooms
½ cup quick-cooking barley
½ teaspoon dried thyme
    leaves
¼ teaspoon dried rosemary
    leaves
¼ teaspoon dried marjoram
    leaves
¼ teaspoon salt*

4 servings

Remove excess fat from
chicken. Sprinkle cavity of
chicken with pepper. Place
onion in cavity. Secure legs
together with string. Set aside.

In 3-quart casserole, combine
remaining ingredients. Mix well.
Place chicken in same casserole.
Cover. Microwave at High for 25
to 30 minutes, or until juices run
clear, rotating dish and stirring
twice. Skim fat from broth. Cut
chicken into pieces and serve
with broth or remove chicken
from bones and add to broth.

*To reduce sodium omit salt.

Per Serving:	
Calories:	367
Protein:	46 g.
Carbohydrate:	28 g.
Fat:	8 g.
Cholesterol:	157 mg.
Sodium:	304 mg.
Calcium:	—
Exchanges:	1 starch, 4 lean meat, 2½ vegetable

Bran Crepes

½ cup unbleached
    all-purpose flour
⅓ cup granular bran cereal
⅛ teaspoon salt*
1⅓ cups skim milk
2 eggs
1 tablespoon reduced-calorie
    margarine
    Vegetable cooking spray

16 6-inch crepes

In medium mixing bowl, combine
flour, cereal and salt. Add milk
and eggs. Mix well. Place
margarine in small bowl. Microwave at 70% (Medium High) for
15 to 20 seconds, or just until
margarine melts. Add to flour
mixture. Mix well. Cover. Chill
for at least 1 hour. Stir until
batter is smooth.

Lightly spray non-stick 6-inch
skillet with vegetable cooking
spray. Heat skillet over medium
heat. Add about 2 tablespoons
batter, tilting to cover bottom of
skillet. Cook until light golden
brown on bottom, about 1
minute. Loosen edge and
carefully turn crepe over. Cook
until light golden brown, about
45 seconds. Cool on wire rack.
Spray skillet before cooking
each crepe. To store crepes,
cool and place each crepe
between two layers of wax
paper. Wrap in plastic wrap
and freeze.

*To reduce sodium omit salt.

Per Serving:	
Calories:	40
Protein:	2 g.
Carbohydrate:	6 g.
Fat:	2 g.
Cholesterol:	35 mg.
Sodium:	54 mg.
Calcium:	38 mg.
Exchanges:	½ starch

Chicken Crepes

½ lb. fresh broccoli, coarsely
   chopped, about 2½ cups
2 tablespoons water
1½ cups cut-up cooked chicken
   or turkey
1 can (8 oz.) water chestnuts,
   drained and sliced
2 tablespoons reduced-calorie
   margarine
2 tablespoons finely chopped
   onion
3 tablespoons all-purpose
   flour
1 teaspoon low-sodium instant
   chicken bouillon granules
¼ teaspoon salt*
¼ teaspoon ground sage
¼ teaspoon dried summer
   savory leaves
⅛ teaspoon pepper
1½ cups skim milk
8 Bran Crepes, page 39
2 tablespoons sliced almonds

4 servings

In 1½-quart casserole, combine broccoli and water. Cover. Microwave at High for 4 to 7 minutes, or until tender-crisp, stirring once. Drain. Stir in chicken and water chestnuts. Set aside.

In 4-cup measure, combine margarine and onion. Cover with plastic wrap. Microwave at 70% (Medium High) for 30 to 45 seconds, or just until margarine melts. Stir in flour, bouillon, salt, sage, summer savory and pepper. Blend in milk. Microwave, uncovered, at High for 4½ to 6½ minutes, or until mixture thickens and bubbles, stirring with a fork 3 or 4 times. Reserve ½ cup sauce. Set aside.

Stir remaining sauce into broccoli and chicken. Spread about ½ cup filling down center of each crepe. Fold opposite sides over filling. Arrange in 10-inch square casserole. Pour reserved sauce over crepes. Sprinkle with almonds. Microwave at 70% (Medium High) for 10 to 13 minutes longer, or until heated through, rotating dish once.

*To reduce sodium omit salt.

Per Serving:			
Calories:	408	Cholesterol:	111 mg.
Protein:	29 g.	Sodium:	394 mg.
Carbohydrate:	31 g.	Calcium:	336 mg.**
Fat:	17 g.	Exchanges:	½ starch, 2 lean meat, 1 vegetable
			1 skim milk, 2 fat

Pasta, Chicken & Broccoli

1½ cups uncooked whole wheat
    elbow macaroni
2 tablespoons lemon juice
2 cups frozen broccoli cuts
⅓ cup chopped onion
1 clove garlic, minced
2 tablespoons water
1½ cups cut-up cooked chicken
¼ teaspoon Italian seasoning
⅛ teaspoon pepper
1 cup low-fat plain yogurt
2 tablespoons grated
    Parmesan cheese
2 tablespoons chopped
    walnuts

6 servings

Prepare macaroni as directed on package, adding 2 tablespoons lemon juice to cooking water. Drain. Set aside.

In 2-quart casserole, combine broccoli, onion, garlic and 2 tablespoons water. Cover. Microwave at High for 6 to 8 minutes, or until tender-crisp, stirring once. Stir in macaroni, chicken, Italian seasoning and pepper. Re-cover. Microwave at High for 3 to 6 minutes longer, or until heated through, stirring once. Blend in yogurt and Parmesan cheese. Sprinkle with walnuts before serving.

Per Serving:	
Calories:	198
Protein:	18 g.
Carbohydrate:	20 g.
Fat:	5 g.
Cholesterol:	30 mg.
Sodium:	397 mg.
Calcium:	136 mg.**
Exchanges:	1 starch, 2 lean meat, 1 vegetable

Curried Chicken

2½ to 3-lb. broiler-fryer chicken, cut into 8 pieces, skin removed
1½ cups buttermilk
2 to 3 teaspoons curry powder
⅛ teaspoon pepper
    Dash ground cinnamon
    Dash ground cloves
1 medium onion, thinly sliced
2 cloves garlic, cut in half
1 cup julienne carrots (1½ × ¼-inch strips)
1 medium potato, cut into ½-inch cubes
1 medium green pepper, cut into chunks
1 cup evaporated skimmed milk
2 tablespoons cornstarch

6 servings

In 3-quart casserole, arrange chicken. In small bowl, blend buttermilk, curry, pepper, cinnamon, cloves, onion and garlic. Pour over chicken, lifting pieces to coat. Cover. Marinate for 30 minutes. Add carrots, potato and green pepper to chicken. Cover. Microwave at High for 20 to 30 minutes, or until vegetables are tender and chicken near bone is no longer pink, turning chicken over and rearranging after half the time. Remove chicken. Remove meat from bones. Cut into bite-size pieces. Set aside. Add milk to vegetable mixture. Remove a small amount of liquid and blend in cornstarch. Stir into vegetable mixture. Microwave at High for 5 to 9 minutes, or until sauce thickens and bubbles. Add chicken to sauce.

Per Serving:
Calories: 186
Protein: 23 g.
Carbohydrate: 15 g.
Fat: 4 g.
Cholesterol: 60 mg.
Sodium: 390 mg.
Calcium: 213 mg.**
Exchanges: 2 lean meat,
                  ½ vegetable, 1 skim milk

Oriental Chicken with Peanut Sauce

1 boneless whole chicken breast (about 12 oz.) skin removed, cut into ½-inch strips
¼ cup sliced green onions
3 tablespoons reduced-sodium soy sauce
2 tablespoons lemon juice
1 teaspoon honey
1 clove garlic, minced
½ teaspoon peeled, grated gingerroot
¼ teaspoon ground coriander
⅛ teaspoon dried crushed red pepper
⅛ teaspoon sesame oil
3 tablespoons unsalted dry roasted peanuts
1 pkg. (3¾ oz.) cellophane noodles
8 oz. fresh spinach, trimmed and torn, about 6 cups
¼ cup shredded carrot

4 servings

Per Serving:	
Calories:	146
Protein:	18 g.
Carbohydrate:	7 g.
Fat:	5 g.
Cholesterol:	34 mg.
Sodium:	237 mg.
Calcium:	94 mg.**
Exchanges:	2 lean meat, 1½ vegetable

How to Microwave Oriental Chicken with Peanut Sauce

Combine chicken and onions in 2-quart casserole. Cover. Set aside. In 2-cup measure, combine soy sauce, lemon juice, honey, garlic, gingerroot, coriander, red pepper and sesame oil. Set aside. Place peanuts in blender; chop until fine particles form. Set aside.

Prepare noodles as directed on package. Keep warm on platter. Microwave chicken and onions at High for 2 to 5 minutes, or until chicken is no longer pink, stirring once. Add spinach. Re-cover. Microwave at High for 2 to 2½ minutes longer, or until spinach wilts. Stir.

Drain cooking liquid into soy sauce mixture. Microwave at High for 2 minutes to blend flavors. Stir in peanuts. Top noodles with chicken and spinach mixture. Pour sauce over chicken and sprinkle with carrot.

Gingered Chicken & Chinese Cabbage

2 tablespoons sliced almonds
2 teaspoons reduced-calorie
　margarine
1 boneless whole chicken
　breast (about 12 oz.) skin
　removed, cut into ½-inch
　strips
2 cups coarsely sliced Chinese
　cabbage
¼ cup chopped carrot
1 can (8 oz.) bamboo shoots,
　rinsed and drained, cut into
　¼-inch strips
⅓ cup sliced green onions,
　½ inch thick

Sauce:

½ cup ready-to-serve
　low-sodium chicken broth
1 tablespoon reduced-sodium
　soy sauce
1 tablespoon sherry
2 teaspoons cornstarch
¼ teaspoon peeled, grated
　gingerroot
¼ teaspoon sugar
⅛ teaspoon chili powder
　Dash cayenne

4 servings

In 1-quart casserole, combine almonds and margarine. Microwave at High for 4 to 5 minutes, or just until almonds begin to brown, stirring once. Set aside. In 2-quart casserole, combine chicken, cabbage and carrot. Cover. Microwave at High for 5 to 7 minutes, or until chicken is no longer pink, stirring twice. Stir in bamboo shoots and onions. Set aside. In 2-cup measure, blend all sauce ingredients. Microwave at High for 2 to 3 minutes, or until mixture bubbles, stirring twice. Stir into chicken. Microwave at High for 2 to 3 minutes longer, or until hot. Top with almonds.

Per Serving:	
Calories:	137
Protein:	16 g.
Carbohydrate:	8 g.
Fat:	5 g.
Cholesterol:	34 mg.
Sodium:	204 mg.
Calcium:	56 mg.
Exchanges:	2 lean meat,
	1½ vegetable

Spicy Chicken Tortillas ▶

Marinade:

- 2 tablespoons reduced-sodium soy sauce
- 2 teaspoons white wine
- 2 teaspoons olive oil
- 1 clove garlic, minced
- 1 teaspoon sugar
- ¼ teaspoon ground cumin
- ⅛ teaspoon cayenne

- 1 boneless whole chicken breast (about 12 oz.) skin removed

Topping:

- 1 medium tomato, seeded and chopped
- ¼ cup chopped green pepper
- 2 tablespoons sliced green onion
- 2 teaspoons red wine vinegar
- ⅛ teaspoon cayenne

- 4 flour tortillas, 8-inch
- ½ cup Tangy Topper, page 27

4 servings

In 1-quart casserole, combine all marinade ingredients. Mix well. Add chicken, turning to coat. Marinate for 30 minutes. In small mixing bowl, combine all topping ingredients. Set aside.

Place chicken breast on roasting rack. Microwave at High for 5 to 8½ minutes, or until chicken is no longer pink, turning chicken over after half the time. Cut into thin strips. Place tortillas between damp paper towels. Microwave at High for 30 seconds to 1 minute, or until warm. Spoon one-fourth of the chicken down center of each tortilla. Add tomato topping and Tangy Topper. Fold in one end of tortilla and then sides.

Per Serving:	
Calories:	202
Protein:	20 g.
Carbohydrate:	20 g.
Fat:	5 g.
Cholesterol:	36 mg.
Sodium:	440 mg.
Calcium:	65 mg.
Exchanges:	1 starch, 2 lean meat, 1 vegetable

Chicken Tacos

- 1 boneless whole chicken breast (about 12 oz.) skin removed, cut into ½-inch cubes
- ¼ cup chopped onion
- 1 clove garlic, minced
- 1 teaspoon lime juice
- ¾ teaspoon ground cumin
- ¼ teaspoon chili powder
- ¼ teaspoon dried oregano leaves
- ¼ teaspoon salt*

- ⅛ teaspoon pepper
- 2 tablespoons no-salt ketchup
- 4 taco shells
  Shredded lettuce
- 1 medium tomato, seeded and chopped
- ½ cup shredded Cheddar cheese
- ¼ cup Tangy Topper, page 27
- ¼ cup Chunky Salsa Sauce, page 26

4 servings

In 1-quart casserole, combine chicken, onion, garlic, lime juice, cumin, chili powder, oregano, salt and pepper. Mix well. Microwave at High for 3 to 4 minutes, or until chicken is no longer pink, stirring after every minute. Stir in ketchup. Spoon one-fourth of the chicken into each taco shell. Top each with lettuce, tomato, Cheddar cheese, Tangy Topper and Chunky Salsa Sauce.

*To reduce sodium omit salt.

Per Serving:			
Calories:	308	Cholesterol:	49 mg.
Protein:	19 g.	Sodium:	302 mg.
Carbohydrate:	20 g.	Calcium:	115 mg.**
Fat:	14 g.	Exchanges:	1 starch, 2 lean meat, 1 vegetable, 2 fat

Chicken Chili ▲

½ cup chopped onion
½ cup chopped green pepper
1 clove garlic, minced
1 can (15½ oz.) kidney beans,
  rinsed and drained
1 can (14½ oz.) no-salt whole
  tomatoes
1 can (8 oz.) no-salt tomato
  sauce
1 can (8 oz.) no-salt whole
  kernel corn, drained
2 tablespoons red wine vinegar
2 tablespoons Worcestershire
  sauce
1 cup cut-up cooked chicken
  or turkey
1 tablespoon packed brown
  sugar
1 teaspoon chili powder
¼ teaspoon dry mustard
⅛ teaspoon pepper

6 servings, 1 cup each

In 2-quart casserole, combine
onion, green pepper and garlic.
Cover. Microwave at High for
2 to 4 minutes, or until tender-
crisp. Add remaining ingredients,
stirring to break apart tomatoes.
Cover. Reduce power to 70%
(Medium High). Microwave for
25 to 30 minutes longer, or until
flavors are blended and chili is
hot, stirring twice.

Per Serving:	
Calories:	187
Protein:	14 g.
Carbohydrate:	22 g.
Fat:	1 g.
Cholesterol:	13 mg.
Sodium:	75 mg.
Calcium:	—
Exchanges:	1 starch, 1½ lean meat, 1 vegetable

Chicken & Vegetable-topped Potatoes

4 medium baking potatoes
1 pkg. (9 oz.) frozen artichoke
  hearts
1 small onion, thinly sliced
1 medium green pepper, cut
  into chunks
2 tablespoons reconstituted
  natural butter-flavored mix
1 teaspoon Worcestershire
  sauce
¼ teaspoon dried thyme leaves
¼ teaspoon dried marjoram
  leaves
¼ teaspoon salt*
1 boneless whole chicken
  breast (about 12 oz.) skin
  removed, cut into ½-inch
  cubes
1 cup sliced fresh mushrooms
1 medium tomato, seeded
  and chopped
2 teaspoons cornstarch
½ cup ready-to-serve
  low-sodium chicken broth
½ cup shredded low-moisture,
  part-skim mozzarella cheese

4 servings

Pierce potatoes with fork. Arrange in circular pattern on paper
towel in oven. Microwave at High for 10 to 14 minutes, or until
tender, turning potatoes over and rearranging after half the time.
Wrap in foil. Set aside.

Unwrap artichoke hearts and place on plate. Microwave at High for
4 minutes, or until defrosted. Break apart and place in 2-quart
casserole. Stir in onion, green pepper, butter-flavored mix,
Worcestershire sauce, thyme, marjoram and salt. Cover. Microwave
at High for 5 to 7 minutes, or until vegetables are tender. Add
chicken, mushrooms and tomato. Mix well. Blend cornstarch and
broth. Add to chicken mixture. Microwave at High for 6 to 13
minutes longer, or until chicken is no longer pink and mixture
thickens, stirring 2 or 3 times. Cut each potato in half lengthwise.
Place 2 halves on each plate. Serve chicken and mozzarella
cheese over potatoes.

*To reduce sodium omit salt.

Per Serving:			
Calories:	357	Cholesterol:	50 mg.
Protein:	28 g.	Sodium:	390 mg.
Carbohydrate:	49 g.	Calcium:	231 mg.**
Fat:	6 g.	Exchanges:	2 starch, 2 lean meat, 4 vegetable

Barbecued Turkey Breast

4½ to 5-lb. bone-in turkey
    breast

Marinade:

  ½ cup reduced-calorie
      Russian dressing
  2 tablespoons Worcestershire
      sauce
  1 tablespoon lemon juice
  ½ teaspoon liquid smoke
  ⅛ teaspoon celery seed
  ⅛ teaspoon pepper

8 servings

Remove gravy package from turkey breast and discard. Place turkey in large plastic food storage bag in baking dish. In 2-cup measure, combine all marinade ingredients. Pour over turkey breast. Secure bag. Marinate in refrigerator for 8 hours or overnight, turning bag occasionally.

Remove turkey breast from marinade, reserving marinade. Place turkey skin-side down on roasting rack. Estimate total cooking time at 12½ to 16½ minutes per pound and divide total cooking time into 4 parts. Microwave at High for first 5 minutes. Reduce power to 50% (Medium). Microwave the remaining first one-fourth of time. Turn turkey on side. Brush with marinade. Microwave at 50% (Medium) for second one-fourth of time. Turn turkey on other side. Brush with marinade. Microwave at 50% (Medium) for third one-fourth of time. Turn turkey skin-side up. Brush with marinade. Microwave the remaining one-fourth of time, or until internal temperature registers 170°F. Let stand, tented with foil, for 10 to 20 minutes before carving.

Per Serving:	
Calories:	200
Protein:	31 g.
Carbohydrate:	1 g.
Fat:	8 g.
Cholesterol:	80 mg.
Sodium:	273 mg.
Calcium:	22 mg.
Exchanges:	4 lean meat

◄ Turkey Wild Rice Paprikash

2 cups cooked wild rice, page 111
2 tablespoons slivered almonds
1 medium onion, thinly sliced
2 tablespoons reconstituted natural butter-flavored mix
¼ cup white wine
2 teaspoons paprika
⅛ teaspoon pepper
12 oz. turkey cutlets
⅓ cup low-fat plain yogurt
¼ teaspoon salt*

4 servings

Prepare wild rice as directed. Stir in almonds. Set aside. In 2-quart casserole, combine onion, butter-flavored mix, white wine, paprika and pepper. Cover. Microwave at High for 4 to 6 minutes, or until onion is tender, stirring after half the time. Add turkey cutlets, turning to coat with onion mixture. Cover with wax paper. Reduce power to 70% (Medium High). Microwave for 5 to 6 minutes longer, or until turkey is no longer pink, turning over and rearranging after half the time.

Place wild rice on serving platter. Remove turkey from cooking liquid and arrange on rice. Stir yogurt and salt into cooking liquid. Spoon sauce over turkey. Reduce power to 50% (Medium). Microwave for 2 to 4 minutes, or until heated.

*To reduce sodium omit salt.

Per Serving:	
Calories:	198
Protein:	13 g.
Carbohydrate:	25 g.
Fat:	3 g.
Cholesterol:	19 mg.
Sodium:	205 mg.
Calcium:	59 mg.
Exchanges:	1½ starch, 2 lean meat

Turkey Parmigiano ►

4 oz. uncooked whole wheat spaghetti
1 can (14½ oz.) no-salt whole tomatoes
1 can (6 oz.) no-salt tomato paste
1 tablespoon snipped fresh parsley
1 teaspoon dried basil leaves
2 cups sliced fresh mushrooms
8 oz. turkey cutlets
2 teaspoons grated Parmesan cheese

4 servings

Prepare spaghetti as directed on package. Drain. Set aside and keep warm. In 9-inch square baking dish, combine tomatoes, tomato paste, parsley and basil. Cover with plastic wrap. Microwave at High for 5 minutes. Stir in mushrooms. Place turkey on tomato mixture. Cover with wax paper. Reduce power to 70% (Medium High). Microwave for 9 to 14 minutes longer, or until turkey is no longer pink, rotating dish once or twice. Serve over cooked spaghetti. Sprinkle with Parmesan cheese.

Per Serving:	
Calories:	193
Protein:	12 g.
Carbohydrate:	34 g.
Fat:	2 g.
Cholesterol:	14 mg.
Sodium:	88 mg.
Calcium:	45 mg.
Exchanges:	2 starch, 1 lean meat, 1 vegetable

Breaded Turkey Cutlets

Coating:

6 tablespoons cornflake crumbs
2 teaspoons snipped fresh parsley
¼ teaspoon dried basil leaves
Dash pepper

12 oz. turkey cutlets
3 tablespoons reduced-calorie Italian dressing
4 medium green pepper rings, ¼ inch thick

4 servings

In shallow bowl, mix all coating ingredients. Dip each cutlet in Italian dressing, then in coating mixture, pressing lightly to coat. Arrange green pepper rings on roasting rack. Place cutlets on pepper rings. Microwave at 70% (Medium High) for 7 to 11 minutes, or until turkey is firm and no longer pink, rotating rack after every 3 minutes.

Per Serving:	
Calories:	112
Protein:	21 g.
Carbohydrate:	5 g.
Fat:	1 g.
Cholesterol:	18 mg.
Sodium:	228 mg.
Calcium:	—
Exchanges:	½ starch, 2 lean meat

Mediterranean Kebabs ▲

Meatballs:

12 oz. ground turkey
  3 tablespoons unseasoned dry
    bread crumbs
  1 egg white
  2 teaspoons dried parsley
    flakes, divided
½ teaspoon onion powder
½ teaspoon dried mint leaves
¼ teaspoon dried rosemary
    leaves, crushed
¼ teaspoon pepper

4 wooden skewers, 10-inch
4 small red potatoes, about
    2½ inches, cut in half
1 medium red or green
    pepper, cut into 16 chunks
1 medium zucchini, cut into 8
    chunks, about 1 inch thick
½ cup reconstituted natural
    butter-flavored mix
¼ teaspoon garlic powder

4 servings

In medium mixing bowl, combine all meatball ingredients using 1 teaspoon parsley. Mix well. Shape into 12 meatballs. Set aside.

For each kebab, assemble potato, red pepper, meatball, red pepper, zucchini, meatball, zucchini, red pepper, meatball, red pepper and potato on skewer. Repeat for remaining kebabs. Place kebabs on roasting rack.

In 1-cup measure, combine butter-flavored mix, 1 teaspoon parsley and garlic powder. Brush kebabs with butter sauce. Cover with wax paper. Microwave at High for 15 to 18 minutes, or until meatballs are firm and potatoes are tender, rotating rack and rearranging kebabs twice. Serve with remaining sauce and couscous, if desired.

Per Serving:			
Calories:	253	Cholesterol:	18 mg.
Protein:	15 g.	Sodium:	274 mg.
Carbohydrate:	36 g.	Calcium:	28 mg.
Fat:	1 g.	Exchanges:	2 starch, 1½ lean meat, 1 vegetable

Easy Herbed Turkey Sandwiches

12 oz. ground turkey
  3 tablespoons unseasoned dry
    bread crumbs
¼ teaspoon fennel seed,
    crushed
¼ teaspoon dried dill weed
⅛ teaspoon garlic powder
⅛ teaspoon salt*
  4 small whole wheat
    hamburger buns
    Shredded lettuce
    Prepared mustard

4 servings

In small mixing bowl, combine turkey, bread crumbs, fennel, dill, garlic powder and salt. Mix well. Shape into 4 patties about ¼ inch thick. Place on roasting rack. Microwave at High for 3 minutes. Turn patties over and rearrange. Microwave for 2 to 4 minutes longer, or just until center is set (some pink juices may remain). Let stand for 2 minutes. Serve in buns with shredded lettuce and mustard.

*To reduce sodium omit salt.

Per Serving:	
Calories:	188
Protein:	16 g.
Carbohydrate:	24 g.
Fat:	3 g.
Cholesterol:	18 mg.
Sodium:	407 mg.
Calcium:	40 mg.
Exchanges:	1½ starch, 2 lean meat

Fruit-stuffed Cornish Hens ▶

2 tablespoons sliced green
    onion
2 tablespoons finely chopped
    celery
2 teaspoons water
½ teaspoon low-sodium instant
    chicken bouillon granules
½ teaspoon poultry seasoning
⅛ teaspoon pepper
1 slice whole wheat bread, torn
    into small pieces
¼ cup chopped dried apricots
¼ cup chopped pitted prunes
1 tablespoon raisins
1 tablespoon chopped almonds
2 Cornish hens, 1½ lbs. each

Glaze:

2 teaspoons dark corn syrup
1 teaspoon reduced-sodium
    soy sauce
  Dash pepper

4 servings

In 1-quart casserole, combine onion, celery, water, bouillon, poultry seasoning and pepper. Cover. Microwave at High for 1 to 2 minutes, or until vegetables are tender-crisp. Stir. Add bread, apricots, prunes, raisins and almonds. Stir.

Fill cavity of Cornish hens with stuffing. Secure legs together with string. In small bowl, blend all glaze ingredients. Brush hens with glaze. Arrange Cornish hens breast-side up on roasting rack. Microwave at High for 17 to 20 minutes, or until legs move freely and juices run clear, rearranging hens once or twice. Brush with any remaining glaze after half the time. Let stand, covered, for 5 minutes.

Per Serving:	
Calories:	311
Protein:	35 g.
Carbohydrate:	21 g.
Fat:	10 g.
Cholesterol:	101 mg.
Sodium:	191 mg.
Calcium:	45 mg.
Exchanges:	1 starch, 4 lean meat, ½ fruit

Barbecued Cornish Hens

2 Cornish hens, 1½ lbs. each
1 small onion, thinly sliced
1 can (8 oz.) no-salt tomato
    sauce
2 tablespoons frozen apple-
    grape juice concentrate

1 teaspoon chili powder
1 teaspoon sugar
1 teaspoon prepared mustard
1 teaspoon olive oil
⅛ teaspoon cayenne

4 servings

Split Cornish hens in half by cutting along breastbone and along either side of backbone. Remove and discard skin and backbone. Set aside.

In 2-quart casserole, combine remaining ingredients. Cover. Microwave at High for 5 minutes, or until mixture boils. Cool slightly. Add Cornish hens, turning to coat with sauce. Cover. Chill for at least 2 hours. Arrange hens on roasting rack with thickest portions toward outside of rack. Cover with wax paper. Microwave at High for 15 to 18 minutes, or until meat near bone is no longer pink, rotating rack and brushing with sauce twice.

Per Serving:			
Calories:	269	Cholesterol:	101 mg.
Protein:	34 g.	Sodium:	135 mg.
Carbohydrate:	10 g.	Calcium:	24 mg.
Fat:	10 g.	Exchanges:	4 lean meat, 2 vegetable

How to Microwave Stuffed Trout

Combine onion, green pepper and margarine in 1½-quart casserole. Cover. Microwave at High for 4 to 5 minutes, or until tender. Stir in tomato, mushrooms, water, buckwheat, salt and celery seed. Re-cover. Microwave at High for 4 minutes, or until hot. Let stand, covered, for 5 minutes.

Stuff each fish with half the vegetable mixture. Arrange fish in 10-inch square casserole with backbones toward outside of dish. Set aside.

Fish & Seafood

◄ Stuffed Trout

1 small onion, thinly sliced
⅓ cup chopped green pepper
1 tablespoon reduced-calorie
 margarine
1 medium tomato, chopped
1 cup sliced fresh mushrooms
3 tablespoons water
2 tablespoons coarse
 buckwheat kernels (kasha)
¼ teaspoon salt*
⅛ teaspoon celery seed

2 trout (6 to 8 oz. each) heads
 removed

Basting Sauce:

2 tablespoons reconstituted
 natural butter-flavored mix
⅛ teaspoon garlic powder
⅛ teaspoon paprika
⅛ teaspoon pepper

4 servings

*To reduce sodium omit salt.

Per Serving:
Calories: 167
Protein: 19 g.
Carbohydrate: 6 g.
Fat: 7 g.
Cholesterol: 49 mg.
Sodium: 215 mg.
Calcium: 50 mg.
Exchanges: 3 lean meat, 1 vegetable

Trout with Toasted Almonds & Garlic

½ cup sliced almonds
2 tablespoons reduced-calorie
 margarine
1 clove garlic, minced
1 tablespoon fresh lemon juice
1 tablespoon snipped fresh
 parsley

⅛ teaspoon cayenne
1 tablespoon white wine
2 trout (6 to 8 oz. each) heads
 removed

4 servings

In small mixing bowl, combine almonds, margarine and garlic. Microwave at High for 4 to 5 minutes, or just until almonds begin to brown, stirring once. Add lemon juice, parsley, cayenne and white wine. Mix well.

Arrange fish in 10-inch square casserole with backbones toward outside of dish. Top each fish with half the almond mixture. Microwave at 70% (Medium High) for 7 to 9 minutes, or until fish flakes easily with fork near backbone, rotating dish after half the time.

Per Serving:
Calories: 226   Cholesterol: 49 mg.
Protein: 20 g.   Sodium: 114 mg.
Carbohydrate: 3 g.   Calcium: 73 mg.
Fat: 15 g.   Exchanges: 3 lean meat, 1 fat

Combine all basting sauce ingredients in small bowl. Brush fish with sauce and drizzle over stuffing. Cover loosely.

Microwave at 70% (Medium High) for 8 to 16 minutes, or until fish flakes easily with fork near backbone, rotating dish once during cooking. Drizzle with remaining sauce before serving.

Salmon Steaks with Lemon Chive Sauce

2 salmon steaks (7 to 8 oz. each) about 1 inch thick

Lemon Chive Sauce:
1 tablespoon reduced-calorie margarine
2 teaspoons finely chopped onion
1 tablespoon all-purpose flour
1 teaspoon freeze-dried chives
⅛ teaspoon salt*
⅛ teaspoon dried summer savory leaves
Dash garlic powder
Dash pepper
¾ cup skim milk
2 teaspoons lemon juice

4 servings

Arrange salmon steaks on roasting rack with thickest portions toward outside of rack. Cover with wax paper. Microwave at 70% (Medium High) for 7 to 10 minutes, or until fish flakes easily with fork, rotating rack once or twice. Let stand, covered, while preparing sauce.

In 4-cup measure, combine margarine and onion. Cover with plastic wrap. Microwave at 70% (Medium High) for 30 seconds to 1 minute, or just until margarine melts. Stir in flour, chives, salt, summer savory, garlic powder and pepper. Blend in milk. Microwave at High for 3 to 5 minutes, or until mixture thickens and bubbles, stirring 3 times. Blend in lemon juice. Serve with salmon steaks.

*To reduce sodium omit salt.

Per Serving:	
Calories:	283
Protein:	27 g.
Carbohydrate:	4 g.
Fat:	19 g.
Cholesterol:	40 mg.
Sodium:	160 mg.
Calcium:	147 mg.**
Exchanges:	4 lean meat, 1 fat

Salmon Steaks & Caper Sauce

2 salmon steaks (7 to 8 oz. each) about 1 inch thick

Caper Sauce:
¼ cup reconstituted natural butter-flavored mix
1 tablespoon capers, rinsed and drained
2 teaspoons snipped fresh parsley
¼ teaspoon onion powder
⅛ teaspoon paprika
⅛ teaspoon pepper

4 servings

Arrange salmon steaks on roasting rack with thickest portions toward outside of rack. Cover with wax paper. Microwave at 70% (Medium High) for 7 to 10 minutes, or until fish flakes easily with fork, rotating rack once or twice. Let stand, covered, while preparing sauce.

In 1-cup measure, combine all caper sauce ingredients. Microwave at High for 30 seconds to 1 minute, or until warm. Serve sauce over salmon.

Per Serving:	
Calories:	283
Protein:	27 g.
Carbohydrate:	4 g.
Fat:	19 g.
Cholesterol:	40 mg.
Sodium:	160 mg.
Calcium:	147 mg.**
Exchanges:	4 lean meat, 1 fat

Oriental Halibut Steaks

Marinade:
¼ cup white wine
2 tablespoons reduced-sodium soy sauce
2 tablespoons unsweetened pineapple juice
1 tablespoon sliced green onion
2 teaspoons vegetable oil
1 clove garlic, minced
¼ teaspoon ground ginger
¼ teaspoon anise seed
⅛ teaspoon hot pepper sauce

2 halibut steaks (10 to 12 oz. each) about 1 inch thick
Fresh parsley

4 servings

In 1-cup measure, mix all marinade ingredients. Place steaks in 9-inch square baking dish with marinade. Cover. Marinate at room temperature, for 30 minutes, turning steaks over once. Arrange on roasting rack. Cover loosely. Discard marinade. Microwave at 70% (Medium High) for 11 to 13 minutes, or until fish flakes easily with fork, rearranging once. Garnish with snipped fresh parsley.

Per Serving:	
Calories:	186
Protein:	27 g.
Carbohydrate:	3 g.
Fat:	5 g.
Cholesterol:	41 mg.
Sodium:	389 mg.
Calcium:	66 mg.
Exchanges:	4 lean meat

Salmon & Parsley-buttered Potatoes ▼

Butter Sauce:

¼ cup reconstituted natural
    butter-favored mix
1 teaspoon snipped fresh
    parsley
⅛ teaspoon ground sage
⅛ teaspoon pepper
    Dash ground nutmeg

12 oz. red potatoes, cut into
    1½-inch chunks
1 medium onion, thinly sliced,
    separated into rings
2 salmon steaks (7 to 8 oz.
    each) about 1 inch thick

4 servings

In 1-cup measure, blend all butter sauce ingredients. Set aside. In 10-inch square casserole, combine potatoes and onion. Pour half of butter sauce over potatoes and onion. Cover. Set remaining sauce aside. Microwave vegetables at High for 7 to 8 minutes, or until potatoes are almost tender, stirring twice.

Arrange vegetables around outside edges of dish. Arrange salmon steaks in center of dish with thickest portions toward outside of dish. Drizzle remaining sauce over salmon and vegetables. Cover. Microwave at 70% (Medium High) for 10 to 15 minutes, or until fish flakes easily with fork, rotating dish twice. Let stand, covered, for 3 minutes.

Per Serving:
Calories:	360
Protein:	27 g.
Carbohydrate:	16 g.
Fat:	20 g.
Cholesterol:	39 mg.
Sodium:	239 mg.
Calcium:	100 mg.**
Exchanges:	1 starch, 4 lean meat, 1½ fat

Salmon & Mushroom Loaf

½ cup sliced fresh mushrooms
½ cup chopped green pepper
¼ cup chopped onion
1 can (15½ oz.) salmon,
    drained and flaked
1 can (10½ oz.) ready-to-serve
    low-sodium cream of
    mushroom soup, divided
½ cup rolled oats
2 tablespoons wheat germ
2 egg whites
1 teaspoon prepared mustard

¼ teaspoon dried basil leaves
¼ teaspoon dried marjoram
    leaves
⅛ teaspoon pepper

Sauce:

    Reserved cream of
    mushroom soup
⅛ teaspoon dried basil leaves
    Dash dried marjoram leaves
    Dash pepper

6 servings

In 1-quart casserole, combine mushrooms, green pepper and onion. Cover. Microwave at High for 2 to 3 minutes, or until tender-crisp, stirring once. Let stand, covered, for 3 minutes. Add salmon, ½ cup mushroom soup, rolled oats, wheat germ, egg whites, mustard, basil, marjoram and pepper. Mix well. Spray 8×4-inch loaf dish with vegetable cooking spray. Spread salmon mixture into prepared dish. Cover with wax paper. Microwave at 50% (Medium) for 16 to 25 minutes, or until center is firm to the touch, rotating dish twice. Let stand, covered, for 5 minutes. Loosen edges and invert onto serving platter.

In small mixing bowl, blend all sauce ingredients. Microwave at High for 1¾ to 2½ minutes, or until hot and bubbly, stirring once. Serve sauce over salmon loaf.

Per Serving:
Calories:	178	Cholesterol:	25 mg.
Protein:	17 g.	Sodium:	390 mg.
Carbohydrate:	10 g.	Calcium:	266 mg.**
Fat:	7 g.	Exchanges:	½ starch, 2 med.-fat meat

Salmon-stuffed Manicotti

8 uncooked manicotti shells
1 can (15½ oz.) salmon,
  drained and flaked
1 cup low-fat cottage cheese
½ cup snipped fresh parsley
¼ cup sliced green onions
1 tablespoon grated Parmesan
  cheese
¼ teaspoon grated lemon peel
⅛ teaspoon dried dill weed
⅛ teaspoon pepper

Sauce:

1 cup low-fat cottage cheese
⅓ cup low-fat plain yogurt
1 tablespoon skim milk
¼ teaspoon dried dill weed
⅛ teaspoon garlic powder

Topping:

1 cup seeded, chopped
  cucumber
1 tablespoon grated Parmesan
  cheese
1 tablespoon snipped fresh
  parsley

4 servings

Per Serving:	
Calories:	372
Protein:	41 g.
Carbohydrate:	27 g.
Fat:	9 g.
Cholesterol:	46 mg.
Sodium:	933 mg.
Calcium:	374 mg.**
Exchanges:	1 starch, 4 lean meat, 1 skim milk

How to Microwave Salmon-stuffed Manicotti

Prepare manicotti as directed on package. Rinse in cold water. Drain. Set aside. In medium mixing bowl, combine remaining ingredients, except sauce and topping. Mix well.

Stuff each manicotti shell with about ¼ cup salmon mixture. Arrange stuffed shells in 10-inch square casserole. Cover with plastic wrap. Set aside.

Combine cottage cheese, yogurt, milk, dill weed and garlic powder in food processor or blender bowl. Process until smooth. Set aside.

Mix cucumber, Parmesan cheese and parsley in small bowl. Mix well. Set aside.

Microwave stuffed shells at High for 5 minutes. Spoon sauce over shells. Re-cover. Reduce power to 50% (Medium). Microwave for 4 to 6 minutes longer, or until heated through, rotating dish once.

Remove to serving platter with slotted spoon. Top with cucumber mixture.

Fish with Fresh Tomato Puree

Tomato Puree:

1 medium tomato, seeded and
   chopped
2 tablespoons no-salt ketchup
1 teaspoon snipped fresh
   parsley
½ teaspoon dried basil leaves
¼ teaspoon onion powder
⅛ teaspoon garlic powder
⅛ teaspoon dried oregano
   leaves
   Dash pepper

12 oz. fish fillets, about ½ inch
   thick, cut into 4 serving-size
   pieces
¼ cup grated Parmesan
   cheese

4 servings

Place all tomato puree ingredients in food processor or blender bowl. Process until smooth. Pour puree into 1-quart casserole. Microwave at High for 5 minutes, or until flavors are blended, stirring once.

Arrange fillets on roasting rack with thickest portions toward outside of rack. Spread tomato puree over fillets. Cover with wax paper. Microwave at High for 4 to 8 minutes, or until fish flakes easily with fork, rotating rack once. Let stand, covered, for 3 minutes. Sprinkle each fillet with Parmesan cheese before serving.

Per Serving:	
Calories:	132
Protein:	18 g.
Carbohydrate:	4 g.
Fat:	11 g.
Cholesterol:	51 mg.
Sodium:	144 mg.
Calcium:	83 mg.**
Exchanges:	2½ lean meat, ½ vegetable

Sole with Spring Vegetables

12 oz. sole fillets, about ¼ inch
    thick, cut into 4 serving-size
    pieces
¼ teaspoon pepper
¼ teaspoon paprika
 1 tablespoon grated
    Parmesan cheese
¼ cup julienne carrot
    (2 × ⅛-inch strips)
¼ cup julienne zucchini
    (2 × ⅛-inch strips)
¼ teaspoon grated lime peel
¼ cup reconstituted natural
    butter-flavored mix

4 servings

Sprinkle one side of each fillet
with pepper, paprika and
Parmesan cheese.

Roll up each fillet with seasoned
side on the inside. Arrange in
9-inch round baking dish, seam
side down. Set aside.

In small mixing bowl, combine
carrot, zucchini, lime peel and
butter-flavored mix. Toss to coat.
Cover. Microwave at High for 2
minutes, stirring once. Spoon
vegetable mixture over fish.
Cover with wax paper. Microwave at High for 5 to 9 minutes
longer, or until fish flakes easily
with fork. Let stand, covered, for
5 minutes before serving.

Per Serving:
Calories:	159
Protein:	16 g.
Carbohydrate:	3 g.
Fat:	9 g.
Cholesterol:	48 mg.
Sodium:	180 mg.
Calcium:	31 mg.
Exchanges:	2½ lean meat,
	½ vegetable

Fillets in Red Wine

3 tablespoons chopped onion
2 tablespoons chopped celery
1 tablespoon reduced-calorie
   margarine
1 clove garlic, minced
2 tablespoons red wine
⅛ teaspoon dried rosemary
   leaves
⅛ teaspoon dried marjoram
   leaves
   Dash pepper
12 oz. fish fillets, about ½ inch
   thick, cut into 4 serving-size
   pieces
½ cup sliced fresh mushrooms
2 teaspoons snipped fresh
   parsley

4 servings

In 9-inch square baking dish, combine onion, celery, margarine and garlic. Cover with plastic wrap. Microwave at High for 2 to 3 minutes, or until tender-crisp. Stir in red wine, rosemary, marjoram and pepper. Arrange fillets with thickest portions toward outside of dish. Spoon vegetables and wine mixture over fillets. Top with mushrooms. Re-cover. Microwave at High for 4 to 8 minutes longer, or until fish flakes easily with fork, rotating dish once. Let stand, covered, for 3 to 4 minutes. Sprinkle with parsley before serving.

Per Serving:	
Calories:	172
Protein:	16 g.
Carbohydrate:	2 g.
Fat:	12 g.
Cholesterol:	47 mg.
Sodium:	78 mg.
Calcium:	17 mg.
Exchanges:	2½ lean meat, 1 fat

Fish with Piquant Topping ▲

12 oz. fish fillets, about ½ inch
   thick, cut into 4 serving-size
   pieces

Topping:
1 can (14½ oz.) no-salt stewed
   tomatoes, drained
2 tablespoons chili sauce

1 tablespoon finely chopped
   onion
2 teaspoons red wine vinegar
¼ teaspoon dry mustard
⅛ teaspoon dried thyme leaves
⅛ teaspoon cayenne

4 servings

Arrange fillets in 9-inch square baking dish with thickest portions toward outside of dish. Set aside.

In small mixing bowl, blend all topping ingredients. Spread over fillets. Cover with plastic wrap. Microwave at High for 5 to 10 minutes, or until fish flakes easily with fork, rotating dish once. Let stand, covered, for 3 minutes.

Per Serving:			
Calories:	177	Cholesterol:	47 mg.
Protein:	16 g.	Sodium:	166 mg.
Carbohydrate:	7 g.	Calcium:	12 mg.
Fat:	9 g.	Exchanges:	2½ lean meat, 1 vegetable

Lemon-Cucumber Fillets ▲

¼ cup Tangy Topper, page 27
¼ teaspoon dried dill weed
⅛ teaspoon grated lemon peel
  Dash garlic powder
12 oz. fish fillets, about ½ inch
    thick, cut into 4 serving-size
    pieces
4 to 8 very thin slices lemon
1 cup seeded julienne
    cucumber (2 × ¼-inch
    strips)

4 servings

In small bowl, combine Tangy
Topper, dill weed, lemon peel
and garlic powder. Mix well.
Cover. Chill at least 30 minutes.
Arrange fillets in 9-inch square
baking dish with thickest
portions toward outside of dish.
Top with lemon slices. Spread
cucumber strips around fish.
Cover with plastic wrap.
Microwave at High for 5 to
8 minutes, or until fish flakes
easily with fork, rotating dish
once. Let stand, covered, for
3 minutes. Serve fillets with
herbed sauce.

Per Serving:	
Calories:	193
Protein:	23 g.
Carbohydrate:	3 g.
Fat:	9 g.
Cholesterol:	50 mg.
Sodium:	72 mg.
Calcium:	73 mg.**
Exchanges:	3 lean meat, ½ vegetable

Easy Baked Fish Fillets

Coating:
3 tablespoons yellow cornmeal
1 tablespoon unseasoned
    dry bread crumbs
1 teaspoon dried parsley
    flakes
½ teaspoon onion powder
½ teaspoon paprika
⅛ teaspoon salt*
  Dash cayenne

12 oz. haddock or halibut fillets,
    about ½ inch thick, cut into
    4 serving-size pieces

Topping:
2 tablespoons reconstituted
    natural butter-flavored mix
2 teaspoons fresh lemon juice

4 servings

On wax paper, mix all coating
ingredients. Dip fillets in
coating, pressing lightly to coat.
Arrange on 12-inch platter or
roasting rack. Microwave at
High for 5 to 8 minutes, or until
fish flakes easily with fork,
rotating once. In small bowl,
blend all topping ingredients.
Drizzle over fish before serving.

*To reduce sodium omit salt.

Per Serving:	
Calories:	179
Protein:	16 g.
Carbohydrate:	8 g.
Fat:	9 g.
Cholesterol:	47 mg.
Sodium:	220 mg.
Calcium:	13 mg.
Exchanges:	½ starch, 2½ lean meat

Spicy Marinated Fillets

1 pkg. (16 oz.) frozen cod or
    haddock fish fillets

Marinade:
⅓ cup low-fat plain yogurt
½ teaspoon grated lime peel
2 teaspoons fresh lime juice
½ teaspoon ground cumin
¼ teaspoon ground coriander
¼ teaspoon paprika
⅛ teaspoon pepper

  Paprika
4 lime wedges (optional)

5 servings

Unwrap frozen fish fillets. Place
on roasting rack. Microwave at
50% (Medium) for 7 to 9
minutes, separating fillets as
soon as possible, rotating rack
once. Let stand for 10 to 15
minutes. In 10-inch square
casserole, blend all marinade
ingredients. Dip fillets in
marinade to coat. Cover. Chill
for 2 to 3 hours. Microwave,
covered, at High for 7 to 11
minutes, or until fish flakes
easily with fork, rotating dish
once. Let stand for 3 minutes.
Sprinkle with paprika and serve
with lime wedges.

Per Serving:	
Calories:	162
Protein:	17 g.
Carbohydrate:	1 g.
Fat:	9 g.
Cholesterol:	50 mg.
Sodium:	59 mg.
Calcium:	39 mg.
Exchanges:	2½ lean meat

◀ Layered Fish Bake

6 uncooked spinach lasagna
   noodles
1 can (14½ oz.) no-salt whole
   tomatoes
1 can (6 oz.) no-salt tomato
   paste
¼ teaspoon fennel seed
¼ teaspoon dried thyme leaves
¼ teaspoon grated lemon peel
⅛ teaspoon cayenne
⅛ teaspoon pepper
1 bay leaf
12 oz. firm fish fillets, about ½
   inch thick
1 carton (15 oz.) part-skim
   ricotta cheese
2 tablespoons snipped fresh
   parsley
2 tablespoons skim milk
1 tablespoon grated Parmesan
   cheese
¼ teaspoon garlic powder
1 can (15½ oz.) salmon,
   drained and flaked
½ cup shredded low-moisture,
   part-skim mozzarella
   cheese

12 servings

```
Per Serving:
  Calories:        236
  Protein:         21 g.
  Carbohydrate:    16 g.
  Fat:             9 g.
  Cholesterol:     44 mg.
  Sodium:          242 mg.
  Calcium:         235 mg.**
  Exchanges:       1 starch, 3 lean meat
```

How to Microwave Layered Fish Bake

Prepare noodles as directed on package. Drain. Set aside. In 2-quart casserole, combine tomatoes, tomato paste, fennel, thyme, lemon peel, cayenne, pepper and bay leaf. Cover. Microwave at High for 10 minutes, stirring once. Set aside.

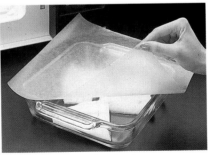

Arrange fish in 9-inch square baking dish with thickest portions toward outside of dish. Cover with wax paper. Microwave at High for 5 to 7 minutes, or until fish flakes easily with fork, rotating dish once. Drain and flake. Set aside.

Combine ricotta cheese, parsley, milk, Parmesan cheese and garlic powder in medium mixing bowl. Remove bay leaf from tomato mixture.

Garlic-Herb Fillets

1 tablespoon water
1 teaspoon grated orange peel
½ teaspoon dried rosemary
  leaves, crushed
¼ teaspoon dried thyme leaves
1 clove garlic, minced
¼ cup snipped fresh parsley
12 oz. fish fillets, about ½ inch
  thick, cut into 4 serving-size
  pieces

4 servings

In small bowl, combine water, orange peel, rosemary, thyme and garlic. Cover with plastic wrap. Microwave at High for 1 minute. Stir in parsley.

Arrange fillets in 9-inch square baking dish with thickest portions toward outside of dish. Top with parsley mixture. Cover with wax paper. Microwave at High for 5 to 7 minutes, or until fish flakes easily with fork, rotating dish once. Let stand, covered, for 3 minutes.

Per Serving:
Calories: 142
Protein: 15 g.
Carbohydrate: —
Fat: 8 g.
Cholesterol: 47 mg.
Sodium: 46 mg.
Calcium: 16 mg.
Exchanges: 2½ lean meat

Florentine Fish Fillets

12 oz. fish fillets, about ½ inch
  thick, cut into 4 serving-size
  pieces
⅛ teaspoon paprika
⅛ teaspoon pepper
1 pkg. (10 oz.) frozen chopped
  spinach
¼ cup shredded carrot

2 tablespoons reduced-calorie
  margarine
¼ teaspoon ground nutmeg
¼ teaspoon ground cinnamon
1 cup cooked wild rice,
  page 111
¼ cup chopped
  water chestnuts

4 servings

Arrange fillets on roasting rack with thickest portions toward outside of rack. Sprinkle with paprika and pepper. Set aside. Unwrap spinach. Place on plate. Microwave at High for 4 to 5 minutes, or until defrosted. Drain thoroughly, pressing to remove excess moisture. Set aside.

In 1-quart casserole, combine carrot, margarine, nutmeg and cinnamon. Cover. Microwave at High for 3 to 4 minutes, or until carrot is tender, stirring once. Add wild rice, water chestnuts and spinach. Mix well. Top each piece of fish with one-fourth of the spinach mixture. Cover with wax paper. Microwave at 70% (Medium High) for 6 to 12 minutes, or until fish flakes easily with fork, rotating rack twice.

Per Serving:
Calories: 252   Cholesterol: 47 mg.
Protein: 20 g.   Sodium: 176 mg.
Carbohydrate: 17 g.   Calcium: 136 mg.**
Fat: 16 g.   Exchanges: 1 starch, 2½ lean meat, ½ vegetable, 1 fat

Place 3 lasagna noodles in bottom of 9-inch square baking dish. Top noodles with half the tomato mixture, half the salmon and half the cooked fish.

Top with half the ricotta cheese mixture and half the mozzarella. Repeat once, ending with the mozzarella cheese.

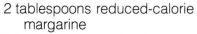

Microwave at 50% (Medium) for 30 to 35 minutes, or until heated through, rotating dish after every 10 minutes. Let stand for 10 minutes.

Scandinavian Poached Fish Salad

Dressing:

½ cup low-fat plain yogurt
1 tablespoon finely chopped
　　red onion
1 tablespoon no-salt ketchup
1 tablespoon sweet pickle
　　relish
⅛ teaspoon pepper

2 medium red potatoes,
　　thinly sliced, about
　　5 oz. each
2 tablespoons water

Seasoning:

2 slices red onion
2 tablespoons white vinegar
1 tablespoon water
⅛ teaspoon whole allspice
⅛ teaspoon whole cloves
⅛ teaspoon whole peppercorns
⅛ teaspoon dill seed

12 oz. firm fish fillets, about
　　½ inch thick, cut into
　　1½-inch chunks
2 cups torn iceberg lettuce
2 cups torn romaine lettuce
1 cup diced pickled beets
1 apple, cut into 8 wedges

4 servings

Per Serving:	
Calories:	330
Protein:	20 g.
Carbohydrate:	43 g.
Fat:	9 g.
Cholesterol:	49 mg.
Sodium:	505 mg.
Calcium:	97 mg.**
Exchanges:	1 starch, 2½ lean meat, 2 vegetable, 1 fruit

How to Microwave Scandinavian Poached Fish Salad

Blend all dressing ingredients in small mixing bowl. Cover. Chill. Place potatoes in 1-quart casserole. Sprinkle with 2 tablespoons water. Cover. Microwave at High for 5 to 7 minutes, or until tender, stirring once. Set aside.

Combine all seasoning ingredients in 2-quart casserole. Gently stir in fish. Cover. Microwave at High for 3½ to 6 minutes, or until fish flakes easily with fork, gently stirring once. Let stand, covered, for 3 minutes. Drain. Chill 1½ hours.

Arrange iceberg and romaine lettuce on large platter. Place fish in center. Surround fish with beets.

Place potato slices and apple wedges around edge of platter. Pour dressing over salad before serving.

Sweet & Sour Fish ▶

12 oz. fish fillets, about ½ inch
    thick, cut into 1½-inch
    pieces
 1 small green pepper, cut into
    ½-inch strips
 1 can (20 oz.) unsweetened
    pineapple chunks, drained
    (reserve juice)
½ cup unsweetened pineapple
    juice
 1 tablespoon reduced-sodium
    soy sauce
 1 tablespoon no-salt ketchup
 1 tablespoon honey
 2 teaspoons cornstarch
 2 teaspoons cider vinegar
⅛ teaspoon garlic powder
⅛ teaspoon ground ginger
⅛ teaspoon pepper
    Dash turmeric
 1 medium tomato, cut into 8
    wedges
 1 tablespoon sliced green
    onion

4 servings

In 2-quart casserole, combine
fish pieces and green pepper.
Cover. Microwave at High for 4
to 7 minutes, or until fish flakes
easily with fork, stirring gently
once. Add pineapple chunks.
Set aside.

Place ½ cup pineapple juice in
1-quart casserole. Stir in soy
sauce, ketchup, honey, cornstarch, vinegar, garlic powder,
ginger, pepper and turmeric
until blended. Microwave at
High for 2½ to 4 minutes, or
until mixture thickens and
bubbles, stirring 2 or 3 times.
Add tomato and onion to fish
and green pepper. Add sauce.
Gently stir to coat. Cover.
Microwave at High for 2 to 4
minutes, or until heated through,
stirring once.

Per Serving:
  Calories: 288
  Protein: 16 g.
  Carbohydrate: 37 g.
  Fat: 9 g.
  Cholesterol: 47 mg.
  Sodium: 196 mg.
  Calcium: 15 mg.
  Exchanges: 2½ lean meat,
                    1 vegetable, 2 fruit

Sunburst Fish Fillets ▶

12 oz. fish fillets, about ½ inch
    thick, cut into 4 serving-size
    pieces
¼ cup dry vermouth
¼ to ½ teaspoon dried
    tarragon leaves
½ medium orange, thinly sliced

4 servings

Arrange fillets in 9-inch square
baking dish with thickest
portions toward outside of dish.
Pour vermouth over fillets.
Sprinkle with tarragon. Top with
orange slices. Cover with wax
paper. Microwave at High for 5
to 8 minutes, or until fish flakes
easily with fork, rotating dish
once. Let stand, covered, for
3 minutes.

Per Serving:
  Calories: 157
  Protein: 15 g.
  Carbohydrate: 4 g.
  Fat: 8 g.
  Cholesterol: 47 mg.
  Sodium: 45 mg.
  Calcium: 18 mg.
  Exchanges: 2½ lean meat

Scallops & Peppers

1 medium green pepper, cut
    into ¼-inch rings
1 medium red pepper, cut into
    ¼-inch rings
1 medium onion, thinly sliced,
    separated into rings
1 cup sliced fresh mushrooms
1 clove garlic, minced
1 tablespoon water
12 oz. scallops, rinsed and
    drained

Sauce:
2 teaspoons cornstarch
1 tablespoon cold water
⅔ cup reserved cooking liquid
1 tablespoon lemon juice
2 teaspoons dry natural
    butter-flavored mix
½ teaspoon low-sodium instant
    chicken bouillon granules
⅛ teaspoon dried crushed red
    pepper

4 servings

Per Serving:			
Calories:	116	Cholesterol:	30 mg.
Protein:	9 g.	Sodium:	348 mg.
Carbohydrate:	13 g.	Calcium:	36 mg.
Fat:	1 g.	Exchanges:	1 lean meat, 2½ vegetable

How to Microwave Scallops & Peppers

Cut green and red pepper rings in half. In 2-quart casserole, combine vegetables, garlic and 1 tablespoon water. Cover. Microwave at High for 7 to 9 minutes, or until tender-crisp, stirring twice. Set aside.

Place scallops in 9-inch square baking dish. Cover with plastic wrap. Microwave at 50% (Medium) for 6 to 9 minutes, or until opaque, stirring twice.

Drain cooked scallop liquid and cooked vegetable liquid into 1-cup measure, adding water if necessary to equal ⅔ cup. Set aside. In 2-quart casserole, combine vegetables with scallops. Cover. Set aside.

Blend cornstarch and water in 2-cup measure. Add remaining sauce ingredients. Mix well.

Microwave at High for 2 to 3½ minutes, or until mixture thickens and bubbles, stirring twice. Pour sauce over scallops and vegetables.

Re-cover. Reduce power to 50% (Medium). Microwave for 3 to 4 minutes longer, or until heated through.

Linguine & Seafood

7 oz. uncooked linguine
4 oz. small shrimp, shelled and deveined*
4 oz. scallops, rinsed and drained*
1½ cups sliced fresh mushrooms
⅓ cup sliced green onions
¼ cup snipped fresh parsley
1 clove garlic, minced
2 tablespoons reconstituted natural butter-flavored mix
Dash cayenne (optional)
3 tablespoons grated Parmesan cheese

4 servings

Prepare linguine as directed on package. Rinse with warm water. Drain. Set aside. In 2-quart casserole, combine remaining ingredients, except Parmesan cheese. Mix well. Cover. Microwave at High for 4 to 7 minutes, or until seafood is opaque, stirring once.

Rinse linguine with hot water. Drain well. Add linguine and cheese to seafood mixture. Toss lightly to mix. Cover. Microwave at High for 1 to 2 minutes, or until hot.

*Cut shrimp and scallops into bite-size pieces, if necessary.

Per Serving:
Calories: 268
Protein: 19 g.
Carbohydrate: 42 g.
Fat: 6 g.
Cholesterol: 33 mg.
Sodium: 228 mg.
Calcium: 100 mg.**
Exchanges: 2 starch, 1½ lean meat, 2 vegetable

Shrimp & Yellow Rice ▶

½ cup chopped onion
1 tablespoon water
2¼ cups hot water
1¼ cups uncooked brown rice
½ medium red pepper, cut into ¼-inch slices
½ medium green pepper, cut into ¼-inch slices
2 teaspoons low-sodium instant chicken bouillon granules
1 teaspoon dried oregano leaves
½ teaspoon turmeric
1 bay leaf
12 oz. small shrimp, shelled and deveined
1 medium tomato, chopped

4 servings

In 3-quart casserole, combine onion and 1 tablespoon water. Cover. Microwave at High for 2 minutes. Add hot water, brown rice, red pepper, green pepper, bouillon, oregano, turmeric and bay leaf. Mix well. Re-cover. Microwave at High for 5 minutes. Reduce power to 50% (Medium). Microwave for 40 to 50 minutes, or until liquid is absorbed and rice is tender. Add shrimp and tomato. Mix well. Re-cover. Microwave at 50% (Medium) for 5 to 8 minutes longer, or until shrimp is opaque, stirring once. Let stand, covered, for 5 minutes. Remove bay leaf before serving.

Per Serving:
Calories: 272
Protein: 20 g.
Carbohydrate: 42 g.
Fat: 3 g.
Cholesterol: 6 mg.
Sodium: 140 mg.
Calcium: 62 mg.
Exchanges: 2 starch, 1½ lean meat, 2 vegetable

◀ Tuna & Pasta

8 oz. uncooked spaghetti
2 tablespoons reduced-calorie
  margarine
¼ cup sliced almonds
1 cup frozen sliced carrots
1 cup thinly sliced zucchini
1 cup sliced fresh mushrooms
¼ cup sliced green onions
½ teaspoon dried basil leaves
¼ teaspoon garlic powder
⅛ teaspoon pepper
1 can (6½ oz.) solid white tuna,
  water pack, drained
¼ cup evaporated skimmed
  milk
3 tablespoons grated Romano
  cheese

8 servings

Prepare spaghetti as directed
on package. Rinse with warm
water. Drain and place in
medium mixing bowl. Set aside.

In 2-quart casserole, combine
margarine and almonds.
Microwave at High for 4 to 5
minutes, or until almonds just
begin to brown, stirring once.
Stir in carrots, zucchini, mushrooms, green onions, basil,
garlic powder and pepper.
Cover. Microwave at High for 6
to 8 minutes, or until vegetables
are tender-crisp, stirring once.
Pour over spaghetti. Stir in tuna,
milk and cheese. Toss to coat.

Per Serving:
Calories: 143
Protein: 6 g.
Carbohydrate: 27 g.
Fat: 2 g.
Cholesterol: 1 mg.
Sodium: 27 mg.
Calcium: 55 mg.
Exchanges: 1 starch, ½ lean meat,
                 2 vegetable

Manhattan Clam Chowder ▲

2 tablespoons reduced-calorie
  margarine
1 cup (¼-inch cubes) potato
⅓ cup chopped onion
¼ cup grated carrot
2 tablespoons snipped fresh
  parsley
2 cans (14½ oz. each) no-salt
  whole tomatoes
1 can (6½ oz.) minced clams
2 tablespoons no-salt ketchup
¼ teaspoon dried thyme leaves
⅛ teaspoon pepper
1 bay leaf

6 servings, 1 cup each

In 2-quart casserole, combine
margarine, potato, onion, carrot
and parsley. Cover. Microwave
at High for 5 to 6 minutes, or
until vegetables are tender,
stirring once. Add remaining
ingredients, stirring to break
apart tomatoes. Cover. Reduce
power to 70% (Medium High).
Microwave for 10 to 14 minutes,
or until heated through, stirring
after half the time. Remove bay
leaf before serving.

Per Serving:
Calories: 105
Protein: 2 g.
Carbohydrate: 13 g.
Fat: 5 g.
Cholesterol: —
Sodium: 60 mg.
Calcium: 44 mg.
Exchanges: ½ starch, ½ lean meat,
                 1 vegetable, ½ fat

Hot Tuna Sprout-Wiches

2 whole wheat English muffins,
  split and toasted
4 thin slices red onion
1 can (6½ oz.) solid white tuna,
  water pack, drained
½ cup alfalfa sprouts
¼ cup low-calorie mayonnaise
1 tablespoon unsalted
  sunflower nuts
1 teaspoon Dijon mustard
⅛ teaspoon celery seed
½ cup shredded Cheddar
  cheese

4 servings

Place muffins toasted side up
on paper towel-lined plate. Top
each with onion slice. Set aside.

In small mixing bowl, combine
tuna, alfalfa sprouts, mayonnaise,
sunflower nuts, mustard and
celery seed. Spread one-fourth
of the tuna mixture on each
muffin half. Top each with one-
fourth of the cheese. Microwave
at 70% (Medium High) for 3 to
4 minutes, or until cheese melts,
rotating plate once.

Per Serving:
Calories: 277
Protein: 19 g.
Carbohydrate: 16 g.
Fat: 15 g.
Cholesterol: 44 mg.
Sodium: 443 mg.
Calcium: 110 mg.**
Exchanges: 1 starch, 2 lean meat,
                 2 fat

How to Microwave Tarragon Beef

Combine all ingredients, except beef, in 2-cup measure. Microwave at High for 2 to 3 minutes, or until mixture boils.

Reduce power to 50% (Medium). Microwave for 1 minute. Cool slightly. Place beef in large plastic food storage bag in baking dish. Pour marinade over beef.

Secure bag. Chill for 4 to 8 hours, turning bag several times.

Beef

Tarragon Beef

1 cup water
3 tablespoons lemon juice
2 tablespoons red wine vinegar
1 tablespoon olive oil
1 teaspoon dried
    tarragon leaves
¼ teaspoon salt*
⅛ teaspoon pepper
1 lb. beef tenderloin

4 servings

*To reduce sodium omit salt.

Per Serving:	
Calories:	252
Protein:	23 g.
Carbohydrate:	1 g.
Fat:	17 g.
Cholesterol:	68 mg.
Sodium:	184 mg.
Calcium:	8 mg.
Exchanges:	3 med.-fat meat

Remove beef. Arrange on roasting rack with thinner portion of beef tucked under for an even shape. Secure with string. Discard marinade.

Shield 1½ to 2 inches on each end of beef with foil. Microwave at High for 3 minutes. Remove foil from beef.

Reduce power to 50% (Medium). Microwave for 5 to 8 minutes longer, or until internal temperature registers 135°F, turning beef over once. Let stand for 3 minutes.

Mandarin Beef ▼

Marinade:

2 tablespoons reduced-sodium
    soy sauce
1 clove garlic, minced
½ teaspoon sugar
¼ to ½ teaspoon finely
    chopped dried hot
    red pepper
⅛ teaspoon ground ginger

½ lb. boneless beef sirloin
    steak, 1 inch thick, cut into
    ⅛-inch strips

Vegetables:

1 can (8 oz.) bamboo shoots,
    rinsed and drained, cut into
    julienne strips
1 medium green pepper, cut
    into ¼-inch strips
½ cup shredded carrot
⅓ cup diagonally sliced green
    onions, 1-inch slices

4 servings

In small mixing bowl, combine all marinade ingredients. Mix well.
Add beef, stirring to coat. Cover. Marinate at room temperature for
15 minutes.

In 2-quart casserole, combine remaining ingredients with beef and
marinade. Cover with wax paper. Microwave at High for 5 to 8
minutes, or until beef is no longer pink and vegetables are
tender-crisp.

Per Serving:				
Calories:	129	Cholesterol:	32 mg.	
Protein:	16 g.	Sodium:	297 mg.	
Carbohydrate:	5 g.	Calcium:	—	
Fat:	5 g.	Exchanges:	2 lean meat, 1 vegetable	

Creole-style Salisbury Steak

1 lb. beef top round steak,
    about ½ inch thick, cut into
    4 serving-size pieces
4 green pepper rings,
    ¼ inch thick
4 slices onion, ¼ inch thick
2 medium yellow squash, cut
    in half lengthwise and
    sliced, about 2 cups
1 can (14½ oz.) no-salt
    stewed tomatoes
2 teaspoons packed
    brown sugar
½ teaspoon dried thyme leaves
¼ teaspoon celery salt*
⅛ teaspoon cayenne

4 servings

Pound beef to ¼-inch thickness.
Place in 3-quart casserole. Top
with green pepper, onion and
squash. In medium mixing bowl,
combine remaining ingredients.
Mix well. Pour over beef and
vegetables. Cover. Microwave
at 50% (Medium) for 1½ to 1¾
hours, or until beef is tender,
turning beef over and basting
with sauce after every 30
minutes. Let stand, covered,
for 10 minutes.

*To reduce sodium omit
celery salt.

Per Serving:	
Calories:	245
Protein:	29 g.
Carbohydrate:	18 g.
Fat:	6 g.
Cholesterol:	69 mg.
Sodium:	176 mg.
Calcium:	39 mg.
Exchanges:	½ starch, 3 lean meat, 2 vegetable

Beef & Bean Casserole ▶

½ lb. boneless beef top round
    steak, trimmed and cut into
    ¾-inch cubes
1 can (15½ oz.) kidney beans,
    rinsed and drained
1 can (10½ oz.) ready-to-serve
    low-sodium French
    onion soup
1 medium onion, cut in half
    lengthwise and thinly sliced
¼ cup snipped fresh parsley
1 clove garlic, minced
½ cup water
¼ cup red wine
2 tablespoons no-salt
    tomato paste
1 teaspoon sugar
½ teaspoon dried
    oregano leaves
¼ teaspoon ground cumin
⅛ teaspoon ground allspice
⅛ teaspoon cayenne

4 servings

In 2-quart casserole, combine
all ingredients. Mix well. Cover.
Microwave at High for 10
minutes. Reduce power to 50%
(Medium). Microwave for 1 to
1¼ hours longer, or until beef is
tender, stirring twice. Let stand,
covered, for 5 minutes.

Per Serving:
Calories:	247
Protein:	22 g.
Carbohydrate:	28 g.
Fat:	5 g.
Cholesterol:	34 mg.
Sodium:	62 mg.
Calcium:	51 mg.
Exchanges:	2 starch, 2 lean meat

Health Loaf

¾ lb. ground round
1 cup shredded carrots
½ cup chopped
    fresh mushrooms
⅓ cup chopped onion
⅓ cup chopped green pepper
¼ cup chopped celery

¼ cup unsalted sunflower nuts
3 tablespoons wheat germ
¼ teaspoon salt*
¼ teaspoon pepper
1 egg
2 tablespoons skim milk

6 servings

In medium mixing bowl, combine all ingredients. Mix well. Spread
into 8 × 4-inch loaf dish. Microwave at 70% (Medium High) for 16 to
24 minutes, or until internal temperature in center registers 150°F,
rotating dish once or twice. Let stand for 5 minutes.

*To reduce sodium omit salt.

Per Serving:
Calories:	164	Cholesterol:	84 mg.
Protein:	16 g.	Sodium:	128 mg.
Carbohydrate:	5 g.	Calcium:	37 mg.
Fat:	10 g.	Exchanges:	2 medium-fat meat, 1 vegetable

Oriental Beef Patties

Topping:
 1 cup shredded cabbage
 ½ cup shredded carrot
 ½ cup fresh bean sprouts
 2 tablespoons finely chopped
    water chestnuts
 2 teaspoons reduced-sodium
    soy sauce
 ⅛ teaspoon five-spice powder
 ⅛ teaspoon salt*

Patties:
 ¾ lb. ground round
 2 tablespoons fine dry
    unseasoned bread crumbs
 1 teaspoon reduced-sodium
    soy sauce
 1 egg white

4 servings

In 1-quart casserole, combine
all topping ingredients. Mix well.
Cover. Microwave at High for
3 to 4 minutes, or until tender-
crisp, stirring once. Set aside.

In small mixing bowl, combine
all patty ingredients. Mix well.
Shape into 4 patties, about ½
inch thick. Arrange on roasting
rack. Microwave at High for 2 to
2½ minutes. Turn patties over.
Microwave for 2 to 3 minutes
longer, or until medium done-
ness. Let stand, covered with
wax paper, for 1 minute. Spoon
topping over patties.

*To reduce sodium omit salt.

Per Serving:	
Calories:	170
Protein:	19 g.
Carbohydrate:	6 g.
Fat:	8 g.
Cholesterol:	58 mg.
Sodium:	268 mg.
Calcium:	28 mg.
Exchanges:	2½ lean meat, 1 vegetable

Southern Burger

 ½ lb. ground round
 1 small onion, chopped
 1 can (14½ oz.) no-salt whole
    tomatoes, drained and
    cut-up
 ½ cup water
 ⅓ cup uncooked long grain
    white rice
 ¼ cup chopped green pepper
 ½ teaspoon dried thyme leaves
 ½ teaspoon salt*
 1 pkg. (10 oz.) frozen
    black-eyed peas

6 servings

In 1½-quart casserole, combine
beef and onion. Microwave at
High for 3 to 4 minutes, or until
beef is no longer pink, stirring
after half the time to break
apart. Drain. Add remaining
ingredients, except peas. Mix
well. Add peas. Cover. Microwave at High for 8 minutes. Stir
to break apart peas. Re-cover.
Microwave at High for 1 to 3
minutes longer, or until mixture
boils. Reduce power to 50%
(Medium). Microwave for 20 to
25 minutes, or until liquid is
absorbed and rice is tender. Let
stand, covered, for 5 minutes.
Stir before serving.

*To reduce sodium omit salt.

Per Serving:	
Calories:	192
Protein:	14 g.
Carbohydrate:	25 g.
Fat:	4 g.
Cholesterol:	26 mg.
Sodium:	196 mg.
Calcium:	24 mg.
Exchanges:	1 starch, 1 med.-fat meat, 2 vegetable

Taco Salad ▶

 ½ lb. ground round
 ¼ cup chopped onion
 1 teaspoon chili powder
 ¼ teaspoon ground cumin
 ¼ teaspoon dried
    oregano leaves
 ¼ teaspoon salt*
 1 can (15½ oz.) kidney beans,
    rinsed and drained
 1 tablespoon reduced-calorie
    Russian dressing
 1 medium tomato, seeded
    and chopped
 4 cups shredded lettuce
 ½ cup Chunky Salsa Sauce,
    page 26
 ¼ cup Tangy Topper, page 27

4 servings

In 1½-quart casserole, combine
beef, onion, chili powder, cumin,
oregano and salt. Microwave at
High for 2½ to 3½ minutes, or
until beef is no longer pink, stirring after half the time to break
apart. Stir in beans, dressing
and tomato. Place 1 cup lettuce
on each plate. Top each with
about 1 cup beef mixture. Spoon
2 tablespoons Chunky Salsa
Sauce and 1 tablespoon Tangy
Topper over each serving.

*To reduce sodium omit salt.

Per Serving:	
Calories:	247
Protein:	22 g.
Carbohydrate:	27 g.
Fat:	6 g.
Cholesterol:	39 mg.
Sodium:	285 mg.
Calcium:	75 mg.**
Exchanges:	1 starch, 2 med.-fat meat, 2 vegetable

74

Rigatoni & Meatballs

7 oz. uncooked rigatoni

Sauce:

4 medium tomatoes, seeded
   and chopped
1 cup sliced fresh mushrooms
1 can (6 oz.) no-salt
   tomato paste
1 teaspoon Italian seasoning
½ teaspoon sugar
⅛ teaspoon salt*
⅛ teaspoon pepper

Meatballs:

1 lb. ground round
1 egg white
2 tablespoons grated
   Parmesan cheese
2 tablespoons seasoned dry
   bread crumbs
2 tablespoons skim milk
¾ teaspoon Italian seasoning
⅛ teaspoon garlic powder
⅛ teaspoon salt*
⅛ teaspoon pepper

⅔ cup shredded low-moisture,
   part-skim mozzarella
   cheese

6 servings

Prepare rigatoni as directed on package. Rinse with warm water. Drain. Set aside.

In 2-quart casserole, combine all sauce ingredients. Cover. Microwave at High for 10 minutes, stirring once. Reduce power to 70% (Medium High). Microwave for 8 to 10 minutes longer, or until flavors are blended, stirring once. Re-cover. Set aside.

In medium mixing bowl, combine all meatball ingredients. Mix well. Shape into 18 meatballs, about 1½ inches. Arrange in 10-inch square casserole. Cover with wax paper. Microwave at High for 5 to 7 minutes, or until firm and no longer pink, rearranging once or twice. Drain. Add rigatoni and sauce. Mix well. Top with mozzarella cheese. Reduce power to 70% (Medium High). Microwave for 1 to 3 minutes longer, or until mozzarella cheese melts. Let stand for 1 minute.

*To reduce sodium omit salt.

Per Serving:			
Calories:	338	Cholesterol:	61 mg.
Protein:	27 g.	Sodium:	259 mg.
Carbohydrate:	35 g.	Calcium:	158 mg.**
Fat:	11 g.	Exchanges:	2 starch, 3 lean meat, 1 vegetable

Dilled Spinach Meatballs

Meatballs:
- 1 pkg. (10 oz.) frozen chopped spinach
- 1 lb. ground round
- ½ cup rolled oats
- ¼ cup finely chopped onion
- 1 egg
- ½ cup skim milk
- ¼ teaspoon dried dill weed
- ¼ teaspoon pepper
- ⅛ teaspoon ground nutmeg

Sauce:
- ½ cup ready-to-serve low-sodium chicken broth
- ¼ cup ready-to-serve low-sodium French onion soup
- 1½ teaspoons cornstarch
- 1 teaspoon dried parsley flakes
- ½ teaspoon dried dill weed
- ¼ teaspoon ground nutmeg
- ¼ teaspoon salt*

8 servings

Unwrap spinach and place on plate. Microwave at High for 4 to 5 minutes, or until defrosted. Press to remove excess moisture.

In medium mixing bowl, combine all meatball ingredients. Mix well. Shape into 32 meatballs, about 1½ inches. Arrange in 10-inch square casserole. Cover with wax paper. Microwave at High for 7 to 11 minutes, or until firm and no longer pink, rearranging once or twice. Drain. Set aside.

In 4-cup measure, blend all sauce ingredients. Microwave at High for 3 to 4 minutes, or until sauce thickens and bubbles. Pour sauce over meatballs.

*To reduce sodium omit salt.

Per Serving:	
Calories:	151
Protein:	15 g.
Carbohydrate:	9 g.
Fat:	6 g.
Cholesterol:	73 mg.
Sodium:	213 mg.
Calcium:	90 mg.**
Exchanges:	1½ med.-fat meat, 2 vegetable

Swedish Meatballs ▼

Meatballs:
- 1 lb. ground round
- ½ cup soft whole wheat bread crumbs
- 2 tablespoons snipped fresh parsley
- 2 tablespoons finely chopped onion
- ¼ teaspoon ground nutmeg
- ⅛ teaspoon ground cinnamon
- ⅛ teaspoon salt*
- ⅛ teaspoon pepper
- 1 egg white
- 2 tablespoons skim milk

Sauce:
- 2 tablespoons reduced-calorie margarine
- 1 tablespoon cornstarch
- 1 tablespoon snipped fresh parsley
- ⅛ teaspoon ground nutmeg
- ⅛ teaspoon salt*
- ½ cup skim milk
- ½ cup ready-to-serve low-sodium chicken broth

6 servings

In medium mixing bowl, combine all meatball ingredients. Mix well. Shape into 18 meatballs, about 1½ inches. Arrange in 9-inch square baking dish. Cover with wax paper. Microwave at High for 4½ to 5½ minutes, or until firm and no longer pink, rearranging once or twice. Drain. Set aside.

For sauce, place margarine in 4-cup measure. Microwave at 70% (Medium High) for 30 seconds, or until margarine softens. Stir in cornstarch, parsley, nutmeg and salt. Blend in milk and broth. Microwave at High for 2½ to 4 minutes, or until sauce thickens, stirring after every minute. Pour over meatballs. Serve with hot cooked noodles, if desired.

*To reduce sodium omit salt.

Per Serving:			
Calories:	180	Cholesterol:	52 mg.
Protein:	18 g.	Sodium:	202 mg.
Carbohydrate:	6 g.	Calcium:	50 mg.
Fat:	12 g.	Exchanges:	2 med.-fat meat, 1 vegetable

Pork

◀ Pork Chops with Bulgur & Bourbon Sauce

1 cup water
¼ cup bulgur or cracked wheat
1 tablespoon chopped almonds
1 tablespoon reduced-calorie
  margarine
⅓ cup chopped celery
⅓ cup chopped apple
¼ cup sliced green onions
1 tablespoon snipped
  fresh parsley
¼ teaspoon ground sage
⅛ teaspoon salt*
⅛ teaspoon pepper

1 teaspoon bourbon
4 butterflied pork chops, about
  ½ inch thick

Sauce:
1 can (10½ oz.) ready-to-serve
  low-sodium cream of
  mushroom soup
1 tablespoon snipped
  fresh parsley
1 tablespoon bourbon
⅛ teaspoon ground sage
⅛ teaspoon pepper

4 servings

Place water in 2-cup measure. Microwave at High for 1½ to 4½ minutes, or until water boils. Place bulgur in small mixing bowl. Add boiling water. Cover and let stand for 30 minutes to soften. Drain and press out excess moisture. Set aside.

In 1-quart casserole, combine almonds and margarine. Microwave at High for 3 to 4 minutes, or just until almonds begin to brown. Add celery, apple, onions, parsley, sage, salt, pepper and bourbon. Mix well. Cover. Microwave at High for 3 to 4 minutes longer, or until vegetables are tender, stirring after half the time. Add bulgur to vegetable mixture. Arrange pork chops in 9-inch square baking dish with thickest portions toward outside of dish. Top each with one-fourth of the bulgur mixture. Set aside.

In medium mixing bowl, combine all sauce ingredients. Mix well. Spoon around chops. Cover with wax paper. Microwave at 70% (Medium High) for 18 to 20 minutes, or until pork is no longer pink, rotating dish after every 5 minutes. Let stand, covered, for 5 minutes.

*To reduce sodium omit salt.

Per Serving:			
Calories:	447	Cholesterol:	73 mg.
Protein:	21 g.	Sodium:	156 mg.
Carbohydrate:	17 g.	Calcium:	37 mg.
Fat:	33 g.	Exchanges:	1 starch, 3 high-fat meat, 2 fat

Hungarian Pork Chops

4 pork loin chops, about
  ½ inch thick
1 small onion, thinly sliced
1 can (8 oz.) no-salt
  tomato sauce
1 teaspoon sugar
1 teaspoon paprika
¼ teaspoon caraway seed
¼ teaspoon celery salt*
¼ teaspoon dried
  marjoram leaves
⅛ teaspoon pepper

4 servings

Arrange pork chops in 9-inch square baking dish with thickest portions toward outside of dish. Top with onion. In small mixing bowl, combine remaining ingredients. Mix well. Pour over chops. Cover. Microwave at 70% (Medium High) for 13 to 15 minutes, or until pork is no longer pink, turning chops over and basting with sauce after half the time. Let stand, covered, for 10 minutes.

*To reduce sodium omit celery salt.

Per Serving:	
Calories:	331
Protein:	20 g.
Carbohydrate:	6 g.
Fat:	25 g.
Cholesterol:	73 mg.
Sodium:	141 mg.
Calcium:	13 mg.
Exchanges:	3 high-fat meat, 1 vegetable

Pork De-lite

1 pkg. (10 oz.) frozen
    asparagus cuts
½ cup chopped onion
¾ lb. butterflied pork chops,
    cut into ⅛-inch strips
1½ cups sliced fresh
    mushrooms

Sauce:

1 tablespoon cornstarch
1 tablespoon cold water
½ cup skim milk
⅓ cup cooking liquid from
    pork and vegetables
½ teaspoon low-sodium instant
    chicken bouillon granules
¼ teaspoon dried
    thyme leaves
¼ teaspoon lemon-pepper
    seasoning
    Dash ground sage

4 servings

Unwrap asparagus and place on plate. Microwave at High for 4 to 6 minutes, or until defrosted. Set aside.

Place onion in 2-quart casserole. Cover. Microwave at High for 2 minutes. Stir in pork, asparagus and mushrooms. Re-cover. Microwave at High for 4½ to 7½ minutes longer, or until pork is no longer pink, stirring after every 2 minutes. Drain pork and vegetables, reserving ⅓ cup liquid for sauce. Set aside.

For sauce, in 2-cup measure, blend cornstarch and water. Stir in milk, ⅓ cup cooking liquid, bouillon, thyme, lemon-pepper and sage. Microwave at High for 2½ to 4 minutes, or until sauce thickens, stirring 2 or 3 times. Stir sauce into pork and vegetables. Microwave at High for 1 minute, if necessary to heat through.

Per Serving:			
Calories:	377	Cholesterol:	74 mg.
Protein:	25 g.	Sodium:	75 mg.
Carbohydrate:	13 g.	Calcium:	85 mg.**
Fat:	26 g.	Exchanges:	3 high-fat meat, 2½ vegetable

Peppered Pork & Rice Casserole

1 cup uncooked brown rice
1 cup uncooked rotini pasta
2 tablespoons reduced-calorie
    margarine
1 clove garlic, minced
1 boneless pork loin chop,
    about 6 oz., cut into ½-inch
    cubes
½ cup chopped low-fat boiled
    ham
⅓ cup sliced green onions
1 small green pepper, cut
    into thin strips
1 medium tomato, seeded
    and chopped
2 cans (10½ oz. each)
    ready-to-serve low-sodium
    chicken broth
¼ to ½ teaspoon ground cumin
¼ teaspoon dried
    oregano leaves
¼ teaspoon salt*
⅛ teaspoon pepper

6 servings

In 3-quart casserole, combine rice, rotini, margarine and garlic. Microwave at High for 5 to 6 minutes, or until rice and rotini are lightly browned, stirring after every 2 minutes. Stir in remaining ingredients. Cover. Microwave at High for 5 minutes. Reduce power to 50% (Medium). Microwave for 40 to 50 minutes longer, or until liquid is absorbed and rice and rotini are tender. Let stand, covered, for 10 minutes.

*To reduce sodium omit salt.

Per Serving:	
Calories:	293
Protein:	13 g.
Carbohydrate:	34 g.
Fat:	12 g.
Cholesterol:	28 mg.
Sodium:	302 mg.
Calcium:	16 mg.
Exchanges:	2 starch, 1 med.-fat meat, 1 vegetable, 1 fat

Coriander Pork Kebabs

Marinade:

¼ cup apple juice
1 tablespoon vegetable oil
1 clove garlic, minced
1 teaspoon ground coriander
½ teaspoon sugar
⅛ teaspoon cayenne
⅛ teaspoon pepper

¾ lb. pork tenderloin, cut into
    20 cubes, about 1 inch
8 whole water chestnuts
4 green onions, white portions
    cut into 8 pieces, about
    2 inches
1 medium carrot
1 medium zucchini, cut into 8
    chunks, about ½ inch thick
8 wooden skewers, 10-inch

4 servings

In medium mixing bowl, combine all marinade ingredients. Mix well. Add pork, water chestnuts and onions. Stir to coat. Chill for 1 hour.

Shave carrot into thin lengthwise strips using vegetable peeler. Wrap carrot strip around each water chestnut. For each kebab, assemble pork, onion, zucchini, pork, water chestnut/carrot, pork, water chestnut/carrot, pork, zucchini, onion and pork on skewer. Repeat for remaining kebabs. Place kebabs on roasting rack. Cover with wax paper. Microwave at 50% (Medium) for 12 to 16 minutes, or until pork is no longer pink, turning kebabs over and rearranging twice. Serve with Garlic Rice & Noodles (page 131), if desired.

Per Serving:	
Calories:	317
Protein:	17 g.
Carbohydrate:	13 g.
Fat:	22 g.
Cholesterol:	58 mg.
Sodium:	356 mg.
Calcium:	45 mg.
Exchanges:	2 high-fat meat, 2½ vegetable, 1 fat

Cantonese Pork & Broccoli

⅓ cup cold water
2 tablespoons
    reduced-sodium
    soy sauce
1 tablespoon white wine
2 teaspoons cornstarch
1 clove garlic, minced
½ teaspoon grated
    orange peel
⅛ teaspoon pepper
¾ lb. fresh broccoli, separated
    into flowerets, stalk
    thinly sliced
¾ lb. pork tenderloin, trimmed
    and thinly sliced
1 can (8 oz.) sliced water
    chestnuts, drained
1⅓ cups hot cooked long grain
    white rice, page 111

4 servings

In 1½-quart casserole, blend water, soy sauce, wine, cornstarch, garlic, orange peel and pepper. Stir in broccoli. Cover. Microwave at High for 3 to 5 minutes, or until broccoli brightens in color, stirring once or twice. Add pork and water chestnuts. Mix well. Re-cover. Microwave at High for 5 to 9 minutes longer, or until pork is no longer pink, stirring twice. Let stand, covered, for 2 minutes. Serve over rice.

Per Serving:	
Calories:	375
Protein:	21 g.
Carbohydrate:	30 g.
Fat:	18 g.
Cholesterol:	58 mg.
Sodium:	556 mg.
Calcium:	163 mg.**
Exchanges:	1½ starch, 2 high-fat meat, 1½ vegetable

Country Pork & Vegetable Stew ▶

1 can (15½ oz.) Great Northern
    beans
1 can (10½ oz.) ready-to-serve
    low-sodium tomato soup
1 can (10½ oz.) ready-to-serve
    low-sodium French
    onion soup
1 pkg. (10 oz.) frozen cut
    green beans
½ teaspoon ground sage
½ teaspoon dried
    marjoram leaves
¼ teaspoon garlic powder
¼ teaspoon salt*
2 bay leaves
1 acorn squash, about 1 lb.,
    peeled, seeded and cut into
    1-inch chunks
¾ lb. butterflied pork chops, cut
    into ¾-inch cubes

8 servings, 1 cup each

In 3-quart casserole, combine all ingredients, except pork. Mix well. Cover. Microwave at High for 25 to 30 minutes, or until squash is tender, stirring 2 or 3 times. Stir in pork. Re-cover. Reduce power to 50% (Medium). Microwave for 5 minutes longer, or until pork is no longer pink. Let stand, covered, for 10 minutes. Remove bay leaves.

*To reduce sodium omit salt.

Per Serving:	
Calories:	192
Protein:	13 g.
Carbohydrate:	22 g.
Fat:	7 g.
Cholesterol:	27 mg.
Sodium:	163 mg.
Calcium:	33 mg.
Exchanges:	1 starch, 1 high-fat meat, 1 vegetable

Ham & Potato Dinner

4 medium baking potatoes
8 oz. fresh mushrooms,
   thinly sliced
2 medium tomatoes, seeded
   and chopped
1 medium onion, cut in half
   lengthwise and thinly
   sliced
¼ cup snipped fresh parsley
3 tablespoons no-salt
   tomato paste
1½ teaspoons low-sodium
   instant chicken
   bouillon granules
¾ teaspoon dried
   marjoram leaves
⅛ teaspoon pepper
6 oz. low-fat boiled ham,
   chopped

4 servings

Pierce potatoes with fork. Arrange in circular pattern on paper towel in oven. Microwave at High for 10 to 14 minutes, or until tender, turning potatoes over and rearranging after half the time. Wrap in foil. Set aside.

In 1½-quart casserole, combine remaining ingredients, except potatoes and ham. Mix well. Cover. Microwave at High for 7 to 10 minutes, or until onion is tender, stirring once or twice. Add ham. Stir. Re-cover. Reduce power to 50% (Medium). Microwave for 2 minutes longer, or until heated through. Cut each potato in half lengthwise. Serve vegetables and ham over potatoes.

Per Serving:			
Calories:	187	Cholesterol:	6 mg.
Protein:	7 g.	Sodium:	163 mg.
Carbohydrate:	35 g.	Calcium:	21 mg.
Fat:	2 g.	Exchanges:	1½ starch, 1 lean meat, 2 vegetable

Pasta & Ham Mornay

1¼ cups uncooked penne
    or mostaccioli pasta
½ cup sliced zucchini,
    ⅛ inch thick
⅓ cup frozen peas
2 tablespoons sliced
    green onion
1 tablespoon reduced-calorie
    margarine
2 teaspoons snipped
    fresh parsley
¼ teaspoon dried basil leaves
    Dash pepper
2 teaspoons all-purpose flour
½ cup evaporated
    skimmed milk
2 tablespoons shredded
    Swiss cheese
1 pkg. (4 oz.) low-fat boiled
    ham, cut into ¼-inch strips

4 servings

Prepare pasta as directed on package. Rinse with warm water. Drain. Set aside.

In 1½-quart casserole, combine zucchini, peas, onion, margarine, parsley, basil and pepper. Cover. Microwave at High for 2 to 3 minutes, or until vegetables are tender-crisp, stirring once. Stir in flour. Blend in milk. Microwave, uncovered, at High for 2½ to 3½ minutes longer, or until mixture thickens and bubbles, stirring once or twice. Stir in Swiss cheese, ham and pasta. Re-cover. Microwave at High for 1 to 3 minutes, or until heated through.

Per Serving:
Calories: 231
Protein: 16 g.
Carbohydrate: 39 g.
Fat: 12 g.
Cholesterol: 21 mg.
Sodium: 510 mg.
Calcium: 152 mg.**
Exchanges: 2 starch, 1 lean meat, 1 vegetable, 1 fat

Meatless

Tomato Cheese Pie

½ cup unbleached all-purpose
    flour
½ cup whole wheat flour
1 tablespoon yellow cornmeal
¼ teaspoon salt*
⅓ cup vegetable shortening
3 to 4 tablespoons ice water

Filling:

1 cup part-skim ricotta cheese
½ cup shredded Cheddar
    cheese
½ cup low-fat cottage cheese
2 eggs, beaten
1 tablespoon all-purpose flour
½ teaspoon dried oregano
    leaves
¼ teaspoon garlic powder

Topping:

1 medium tomato, thinly sliced
1 tablespoon grated Parmesan
    cheese
1 tablespoon snipped fresh
    parsley
¼ teaspoon dried oregano
    leaves

6 servings

In medium mixing bowl, combine all-purpose flour, whole wheat flour, cornmeal and salt. Cut in shortening to form coarse crumbs. Sprinkle with water, 1 tablespoon at a time, mixing with fork until particles are moistened and cling together. Form dough into a ball. Roll out on lightly floured board at least 2 inches larger than inverted 9-inch pie plate. Ease into plate. Trim and flute edge. Prick thoroughly. Microwave at High for 6 to 8 minutes, or until crust appears dry and opaque, rotating plate after every 2 minutes. Set aside.

For filling, in medium mixing bowl, combine all ingredients. Mix well. Spread evenly into prepared crust. Place pie plate on saucer in oven. Microwave at 50% (Medium) for 11 to 19 minutes, or until center is soft-set, rotating plate one-half turn after every 3 minutes. Top with tomato slices. In small bowl, blend all remaining topping ingredients. Sprinkle over tomato slices. Let stand for 10 minutes before serving.

*To reduce sodium omit salt.

Per Serving:			
Calories:	315	Cholesterol:	115 mg.
Protein:	14 g.	Sodium:	308 mg.
Carbohydrate:	20 g.	Calcium:	220 mg.**
Fat:	26 g.	Exchanges:	1 starch, 2 med.-fat meat, 1 vegetable, 2 fat

Spinach Pie

Filling:

2 pkgs. (10 oz. each) frozen
    chopped spinach
¾ cup part-skim ricotta cheese
½ cup evaporated skimmed
    milk
¼ cup chopped
    water chestnuts
1 egg
1 egg yolk
2 teaspoons cider vinegar
¾ teaspoon dried basil leaves
¼ teaspoon ground nutmeg

Crust:

2 cups cooked brown rice,
    page 111
1 egg white
3 tablespoons grated
    Parmesan cheese

4 servings

Unwrap spinach. Place on plate. Microwave at High for 6 to 8 minutes, or until defrosted, rotating plate once. Drain. Press to remove excess moisture. In medium mixing bowl, combine spinach and remaining filling ingredients. Mix well. Set aside.

In small mixing bowl, combine all crust ingredients. Mix well. Press firmly against bottom and sides of 9-inch pie plate. Microwave at High for 4 to 7 minutes, or until center is set, rotating plate once.

Spread filling evenly into rice crust. Microwave at High for 5 minutes. Reduce power to 50% (Medium). Microwave for 15 to 25 minutes longer, or until center is firm to touch, rotating plate once or twice. Let stand for 3 minutes.

Per Serving:	
Calories:	285
Protein:	18 g.
Carbohydrate:	39 g.
Fat:	8 g.
Cholesterol:	87 mg.
Sodium:	320 mg.
Calcium:	509 mg.**
Exchanges:	1½ starch, 1 med.-fat meat, 2 vegetable, ½ skim milk

Tofu Vegetable Sauté ▲

1 cup uncooked couscous
1 pkg. (10 oz.) frozen
    asparagus cuts
1 lb. tofu, rinsed and cut into
    ¾-inch cubes
2 cups sliced fresh mushrooms
1 can (8 oz.) bamboo shoots,
    rinsed and drained
½ cup thinly sliced green
    onions
¼ cup reduced-sodium soy
    sauce

1 tablespoon cornstarch
1 tablespoon white wine
1 clove garlic, minced
2 teaspoons vegetable oil
1 teaspoon sugar
¼ teaspoon peeled, minced
    gingerroot
¼ teaspoon sesame oil
⅛ teaspoon cayenne

4 servings

Prepare couscous as directed on package. Set aside. Unwrap asparagus. Place on plate. Microwave at High for 4 to 5 minutes, or until defrosted. Stir to break apart. In 3-quart casserole, combine asparagus, tofu, mushrooms, bamboo shoots and onions. Set aside.

In small mixing bowl, blend remaining ingredients, except couscous. Pour over tofu and vegetable mixture. Stir to coat. Cover. Microwave at High for 12 to 13 minutes, or until sauce thickens and is translucent, stirring after every 4 minutes. Serve over couscous.

Per Serving:			
Calories:	295	Cholesterol:	—
Protein:	17 g.	Sodium:	523 mg.
Carbohydrate:	41 g.	Calcium:	178 mg.**
Fat:	9 g.	Exchanges:	2 starch, 1 lean meat, 2 vegetable, 1 fat

Vegetable Curry

1 medium onion, cut into
  ½-inch pieces
1 medium green pepper, cut
  into thin strips
1 small red baking apple,
  cored and chopped
½ cup thinly sliced carrot
1 clove garlic, minced
2 tablespoons reduced-calorie
  margarine
1 can (16 oz.) pinto beans,
  rinsed and drained
1 medium tomato, seeded
  and chopped
¼ cup raisins
1 tablespoon olive oil
1½ teaspoons curry powder
½ teaspoon salt*
¼ teaspoon dried dill weed
¼ teaspoon pepper
2 cups cooked brown rice,
  page 111
1 tablespoon unsalted
  sunflower nuts

4 servings

In 2-quart casserole, combine
onion, green pepper, apple,
carrot, garlic and margarine.
Cover. Microwave at High for 6
to 10 minutes, or until onion and
carrot are tender, stirring after
every 2 minutes. Add remaining
ingredients, except rice and
sunflower nuts. Mix well.
Re-cover. Microwave at High for
6 to 7 minutes longer, or until
heated through and flavors are
blended. Serve over brown rice.
Sprinkle with sunflower nuts.

*To reduce sodium omit salt.

Per Serving:	
Calories:	342
Protein:	9 g.
Carbohydrate:	45 g.
Fat:	14 g.
Cholesterol:	—
Sodium:	442 mg.
Calcium:	29 mg.
Exchanges:	2 starch, 1 vegetable, ½ fruit, 3 fat

How to Microwave Middle Eastern Cabbage

Combine cabbage and water in 2-quart casserole. Cover with plastic wrap. Microwave at High for 6 to 9 minutes, or until outer leaves are pliable, rotating dish once. Drain. Cool slightly.

Place cooled cabbage on 2 crisscrossed sheets of plastic wrap. Gently pull back pliable outer leaves. Cut out inside of cabbage, leaving outer leaves attached to stem. Chop enough cabbage to equal 1 cup.

Combine chopped cabbage, tomato and onions in 2-quart casserole. Cover. Microwave at High for 2 to 3 minutes, or until cabbage is tender-crisp. Stir in remaining ingredients, except lemon wedges. Mix well.

Middle Eastern Cabbage

1 medium head cabbage,
  about 2 lbs.
½ cup water
1 medium tomato, seeded and
  chopped
3 tablespoons sliced green
  onions
2 cups cooked brown rice,
  page 111
¼ cup wheat germ
¼ cup chopped almonds
1 egg
1 tablespoon lemon juice
½ teaspoon ground cinnamon
½ teaspoon salt*
⅛ teaspoon pepper
⅛ teaspoon ground allspice
⅛ teaspoon ground ginger
4 lemon wedges

4 servings

*To reduce sodium omit salt.

Per Serving:	
Calories:	221
Protein:	9 g.
Carbohydrate:	32 g.
Fat:	8 g.
Cholesterol:	69 mg.
Sodium:	284 mg.
Calcium:	69 mg.
Exchanges:	1½ starch, 2 vegetable, 1½ fat

One-Dish Garbanzo Bake

2¼ cups water
¾ cup bulgur or cracked
  wheat
1 small green pepper, cut into
  1-inch chunks
1 small onion, thinly sliced
  and separated into rings
1 parsnip, cut into ½-inch
  cubes, about ¾ cup,
  discard woody core
1 tablespoon olive oil
1 can (15 oz.) garbanzo
  beans, rinsed and drained
1 can (8 oz.) no-salt tomato
  sauce
½ cup thinly sliced yellow
  squash
⅓ cup water
¼ teaspoon dried rosemary
  leaves
¼ teaspoon salt*
⅛ teaspoon pepper

4 servings

Place 2¼ cups water in 4-cup
measure. Microwave at High for
4 to 6 minutes, or until water
boils. Place bulgur in small
mixing bowl. Add boiling water.
Cover and let stand for 30
minutes to soften. Drain and
press to remove excess
moisture. Set aside.

In 2-quart casserole, combine
green pepper, onion, parsnip
and olive oil. Cover. Microwave
at High for 4 to 5 minutes, or
until tender-crisp, stirring once.
Stir in remaining ingredients,
except bulgur. Re-cover. Microwave at High for 9 to 14
minutes longer, or until vegetables are tender, stirring twice.
Let stand, covered, for 5
minutes. Serve over bulgur,
if desired.

*To reduce sodium omit salt.

Per Serving:	
Calories:	230
Protein:	9 g.
Carbohydrate:	37 g.
Fat:	6 g.
Cholesterol:	—
Sodium:	579 mg.
Calcium:	24 mg.
Exchanges:	2 starch, 1½ vegetable, 1 fat

Lift cabbage leaves and plastic
wrap and place in deep bowl or
2-quart measure. Spoon stuffing
into cabbage shell. Gently pull
leaves toward center to enclose
stuffing. Secure plastic wrap
tightly around cabbage.

Microwave at High for 7 to 10
minutes, or until internal
temperature in center registers
140°F. Let stand, covered, for 5
minutes. Cut cabbage into
wedges. Squeeze lemon juice
over each serving.

Simmered Beans & Artichokes ▲

3 cups water
1 cup bulgur or cracked wheat
1 pkg. (9 oz.) frozen artichoke
   hearts
½ cup coarsely chopped onion
½ cup coarsely chopped green
   pepper
1 clove garlic, minced
1 tablespoon olive oil
1 can (16 oz.) Great Northern
   beans, rinsed and drained
1 can (14½ oz.) no-salt stewed
   tomatoes

½ cup white wine
1 tablespoon packed brown
   sugar
¼ teaspoon salt*
¼ teaspoon dried oregano
   leaves
⅛ teaspoon dried marjoram
   leaves
1 medium white potato, cut in
   half lengthwise and sliced
   ¼ inch thick

6 servings

Place water in 4-cup measure. Microwave at High for 5½ to 7½ minutes, or until water boils. Place bulgur in medium mixing bowl. Add boiling water. Cover and let stand for 30 minutes to soften. Drain and press out excess moisture. Set aside.

In 2-quart casserole, combine artichoke hearts, onion, green pepper, garlic and olive oil. Cover. Microwave at High for 6 to 9 minutes, or until onion is tender-crisp, stirring once. Stir in remaining ingredients, except bulgur and potato. Re-cover. Microwave at High for 5 to 8 minutes, or until bubbly around edges. Stir in potato. Re-cover. Microwave at High for 15 to 25 minutes longer, or until potato is tender, stirring twice. Serve over bulgur, if desired.

*To reduce sodium omit salt.

Per Serving:			
Calories:	281	Cholesterol:	—
Protein:	9 g.	Sodium:	122 mg.
Carbohydrate:	53 g.	Calcium:	35 mg.
Fat:	3 g.	Exchanges:	3 starch, 1½ vegetable, ½ fat

Cuban Black Beans

2 cups chopped onions
1 medium green pepper,
   chopped
2 cloves garlic, minced
2 tablespoons olive oil
5 cups hot water
1 lb. dried black beans,
   rinsed and drained
3 tablespoons red wine
   vinegar
1½ teaspoons dried oregano
   leaves
½ teaspoon dried basil leaves
½ teaspoon dried marjoram
   leaves
½ teaspoon salt*
⅛ teaspoon dried crushed red
   pepper
2 bay leaves
3 cups hot cooked rice,
   page 111

Topping:
⅓ cup chopped onion
   Red wine vinegar

6 servings, about 1 cup each

In deep 3-quart casserole, combine onions, green pepper, garlic and olive oil. Stir. Cover. Microwave at High for 5 to 7 minutes, or until tender-crisp, stirring once. Add remaining ingredients, except rice and topping. Stir. Re-cover. Micro-wave at High for 10 minutes. Reduce power to 50% (Medium). Microwave for 1½ hours, or until beans are tender, stirring once or twice. Microwave, uncovered, at High for 10 to 30 minutes longer, or until thick. Remove bay leaves. Serve over rice. Top each serving with onion and vinegar.

*To reduce sodium omit salt.

Per Serving:	
Calories:	352
Protein:	15 g.
Carbohydrate:	63 g.
Fat:	6 g.
Cholesterol:	—
Sodium:	549 mg.
Calcium:	68 mg.
Exchanges:	3½ starch, 2 vegetable, 1 fat

Red Beans & Rice ▼

6 cups hot water
1 lb. dried kidney beans, rinsed and drained
1 cup chopped onions
1 medium green pepper, chopped
1 tablespoon Worcestershire sauce
1½ teaspoons dried summer savory leaves
½ teaspoon dried thyme leaves
½ teaspoon salt*
¼ teaspoon hot pepper sauce
⅛ teaspoon garlic powder
⅛ teaspoon pepper
1 can (8 oz.) no-salt tomato sauce
1 tablespoon cider vinegar
4 cups hot cooked rice, page 111

8 servings, ¾ cup each

In 5-quart casserole, combine all ingredients, except tomato sauce, vinegar and rice. Mix well. Cover. Microwave at High for 10 minutes. Reduce power to 50% (Medium). Microwave for 1¾ to 2¼ hours, or until beans are tender, stirring gently after every 30 minutes. Add additional water if necessary, to keep beans just covered during cooking. Stir in tomato sauce and vinegar. Microwave, uncovered, at High for 10 to 25 minutes longer, or until desired consistency, stirring occasionally. Serve over rice.

*To reduce sodium omit salt.

Per Serving:	
Calories:	288
Protein:	13 g.
Carbohydrate:	48 g.
Fat:	1 g.
Cholesterol:	—
Sodium:	170 mg.
Calcium:	67 mg.
Exchanges:	3 starch, ½ lean meat, ½ vegetable

Navy Beans in Lemony Dijon Sauce

6 cups hot water
1 lb. dried navy beans, rinsed and drained
1 medium onion, chopped
½ cup chopped carrot
½ cup chopped celery
2 tablespoons snipped fresh parsley
½ teaspoon dried dill weed
¼ teaspoon salt*
⅛ teaspoon fennel seed
½ cup cooking liquid from beans
¼ cup reconstituted natural butter-flavored mix
3 tablespoons lemon juice
2 tablespoons Dijon mustard
2 tablespoons honey
¾ teaspoon lemon-pepper seasoning
¼ teaspoon dried basil leaves
1 cup uncooked couscous

8 servings, ¾ cup each

In 5-quart casserole, combine water, beans, onion, carrot, celery, parsley, dill, salt and fennel. Cover. Microwave at High for 10 minutes. Reduce power to 50% (Medium). Microwave for 1¾ to 2¼ hours, or until beans are tender, stirring twice. Drain, reserving ½ cup cooking liquid. Return beans and reserved cooking liquid to same 5-quart casserole. Stir in remaining ingredients, except couscous. Microwave, uncovered, at 50% (Medium) for 5 to 8 minutes longer, or until heated through and flavors are blended, stirring once. Prepare couscous as directed on package. Serve over couscous.

*To reduce sodium omit salt.

Per Serving:			
Calories:	279	Cholesterol:	—
Protein:	13 g.	Sodium:	230 mg.
Carbohydrate:	50 g.	Calcium:	87 mg.**
Fat:	5 g.	Exchanges:	3 starch, 1 vegetable, 1 fat

Split Peas & Lentils

5 cups hot water
½ cup dried green split peas, rinsed and drained
½ cup dried lentils, rinsed and drained
½ cup chopped onion
1 tablespoon dried sweet pepper flakes
1 tablespoon olive oil
½ teaspoon dried parsley flakes
½ teaspoon dried oregano leaves
½ teaspoon salt*
⅛ teaspoon pepper
⅛ teaspoon instant minced garlic
1 bay leaf
1 cup (½-inch cubes) white potato
⅓ cup thinly sliced carrot

4 servings, 1 cup each

In 3-quart casserole, combine all ingredients, except potato and carrot. Mix well. Cover. Microwave at High for 40 minutes, stirring twice. Add potato and carrot. Re-cover. Microwave at High for 10 to 15 minutes longer, or until vegetables are tender, stirring twice. Remove bay leaf.

*To reduce sodium omit salt.

Per Serving:
Calories: 326
Protein: 19 g.
Carbohydrate: 57 g.
Fat: 4 g.
Cholesterol: —
Sodium: 293 mg.
Calcium: 52 mg.
Exchanges: 3 starch, 1 lean meat, 2 vegetable

Herbed Summer Stew

1 can (16 oz.) Great Northern beans, rinsed and drained
1 can (16 oz.) pinto beans, rinsed and drained
2 cups sliced yellow squash, ¼ inch thick
1½ cups frozen cut green beans
1½ cups sliced fresh mushrooms
1 medium onion, thinly sliced
1½ cups cooked brown rice, page 111
1 can (10½ oz.) ready-to-serve low-sodium chicken broth
¼ cup white wine
2 teaspoons olive oil
2 teaspoons white wine vinegar
1 teaspoon dried basil leaves
½ teaspoon dried marjoram leaves

4 servings, 2 cups each

In 3-quart casserole, combine all ingredients. Mix well. Cover. Microwave at High for 15 to 20 minutes, or until hot and flavors are blended, stirring 2 or 3 times.

Per Serving:
Calories: 422
Protein: 21 g.
Carbohydrate: 74 g.
Fat: 6 g.
Cholesterol: 4 mg.
Sodium: 185 mg.
Calcium: 102 mg.**
Exchanges: 4 starch, 3 vegetable, 1 fat

Hearty Minestrone ▶

1 medium onion, thinly sliced
1 tablespoon olive oil
⅛ teaspoon instant minced garlic
1 can (14½ oz.) no-salt whole tomatoes, cut-up
1 pkg. (10 oz.) frozen mixed vegetables
1 cup cooked Great Northern beans, page 110
1 cup no-salt tomato juice
1 cup water
½ cup cooked brown rice, page 111
1 medium zucchini, sliced ¼ inch thick
1½ teaspoons sugar
1 teaspoon low-sodium instant beef bouillon granules
1 teaspoon Italian seasoning
⅛ teaspoon pepper
1 cup hot cooked whole wheat elbow macaroni
¼ cup grated Parmesan cheese

4 servings, 2 cups each

In 3-quart casserole, combine onion, olive oil and garlic. Cover. Microwave at High for 5 to 7 minutes, or until onion is tender. Stir in remaining ingredients, except macaroni and Parmesan cheese. Re-cover. Microwave at High for 15 to 22 minutes longer, or until zucchini is tender, stirring twice. Stir in macaroni. Sprinkle with Parmesan cheese.

Per Serving:
Calories: 316
Protein: 15 g.
Carbohydrate: 54 g.
Fat: 7 g.
Cholesterol: 5 mg.
Sodium: 189 mg.
Calcium: 169 mg.**
Exchanges: 3 starch, 2 vegetable, 1 fat

Ratatouille Potatoes

4 medium baking potatoes
1 eggplant, about 1¼ lbs.,
   peeled and chopped
1 can (14½ oz.) no-salt whole
   tomatoes
1 medium green pepper, cut
   into 1-inch chunks
⅓ cup chopped onion
2 tablespoons no-salt tomato
   paste
2 tablespoons olive oil
½ teaspoon dried thyme leaves
½ teaspoon dried oregano
   leaves
¼ teaspoon dried rosemary
   leaves
¼ teaspoon garlic powder
¼ teaspoon salt*
¼ teaspoon pepper
2 tablespoons grated Romano
   cheese
1 cup shredded Swiss cheese

4 servings

Pierce potatoes with fork. Arrange in circular pattern on paper towel in oven. Microwave at High for 10 to 14 minutes, or until tender, turning potatoes over and rearranging after half the time. Wrap in foil. Set aside.

In 3-quart casserole, combine remaining ingredients, except Romano and Swiss cheeses and potatoes. Cover. Microwave at High for 18 to 24 minutes, or until eggplant is tender, stirring after every 5 minutes. Stir in Romano cheese.

Cut each potato in half lengthwise. Place on large platter. Top with ratatouille. Sprinkle with Swiss cheese. Microwave at 70% (Medium High) for 2 to 4 minutes, or until cheese melts.

*To reduce sodium omit salt.

Per Serving:			
Calories:	378	Cholesterol:	28 mg.
Protein:	15 g.	Sodium:	270 mg.
Carbohydrate:	47 g.	Calcium:	319 mg.**
Fat:	16 g.	Exchanges:	2½ starch, ½ high-fat meat, 2 vegetable, 2 fat

Triple Cheese-Vegetable Potatoes

4 medium baking potatoes
1 pkg. (10 oz.) frozen
    asparagus cuts
½ cup frozen peas
2 tablespoons water
1¼ cups part-skim ricotta
    cheese
½ cup shredded low-moisture,
    part-skim mozzarella
    cheese
⅓ cup shredded Cheddar
    cheese
3 tablespoons evaporated
    skimmed milk
1 tablespoon snipped fresh
    parsley
¼ to ½ teaspoon onion
    powder
¼ teaspoon dried basil leaves
¼ teaspoon salt*
⅛ teaspoon pepper
    Paprika

4 servings

Pierce potatoes with fork. Arrange in circular pattern on paper towel in oven. Microwave at High for 10 to 14 minutes, or until tender, turning potatoes over and rearranging after half the time. Wrap in foil. Set aside.

In 1-quart casserole, combine asparagus, peas and water. Cover. Microwave at High for 6 to 9 minutes, or until hot, stirring once. Drain. Cover. Set aside. In medium mixing bowl, blend remaining ingredients, except potatoes, asparagus and peas. Stir in asparagus and peas. Cut each potato in half lengthwise. Place on large platter. Top with vegetable-cheese mixture. Microwave at 70% (Medium High) for 7 to 12 minutes, or until hot, rotating platter once or twice.

*To reduce sodium omit salt.

Per Serving:			
Calories:	385	Cholesterol:	42 mg.
Protein:	23 g.	Sodium:	385 mg.
Carbohydrate:	48 g.	Calcium:	452 mg.**
Fat:	12 g.	Exchanges:	2½ starch, 1½ high-fat meat, 2 vegetable

Vegetable Rarebit Potatoes

4 medium baking potatoes
1 pkg. (10 oz.) frozen baby
    lima beans
¼ cup water
1 pkg. (10 oz.) frozen
    chopped broccoli
3 tablespoons all-purpose
    flour
2 tablespoons reconstituted
    natural butter-flavored mix
1 teaspoon prepared mustard
½ teaspoon low-sodium instant
    chicken bouillon granules
¼ teaspoon salt*
⅛ teaspoon pepper
1⅓ cups skim milk
1 cup shredded pasteurized
    process American cheese
½ cup sliced fresh mushrooms

4 servings

Pierce potatoes with fork. Arrange in circular pattern on paper towel in oven. Microwave at High for 10 to 14 minutes, or until tender, turning potatoes over and rearranging after half the time. Wrap in foil. Set aside.

In 2-quart casserole, combine lima beans and water. Cover. Microwave at High for 3 minutes. Add broccoli. Re-cover. Microwave at High for 7 to 12 minutes longer, or until broccoli is tender-crisp, stirring twice. Drain. Cover. Set aside. In 4-cup measure, blend flour, butter-flavored mix, mustard, bouillon, salt and pepper. Blend in milk. Microwave at High for 5 to 6½ minutes, or until sauce thickens and bubbles, stirring twice. Stir in American cheese until cheese melts. Add cheese sauce and mushrooms to vegetables in same 2-quart casserole. Stir. Microwave, uncovered, at High for 4 to 5 minutes, or until mushrooms are tender and mixture is hot. Cut each potato in half lengthwise. Serve vegetables and sauce over potatoes.

*To reduce sodium omit salt.

Per Serving:			
Calories:	340	Cholesterol:	32 mg.
Protein:	23 g.	Sodium:	494 mg.
Carbohydrate:	42 g.	Calcium:	409 mg.**
Fat:	10 g.	Exchanges:	2 starch, 2 med.-fat meat, 2 vegetable

Potato & Cabbage Au Gratin ▲

¼ cup reconstituted natural
   butter-flavored mix
3 tablespoons all-purpose
   flour
2 tablespoons finely chopped
   green onion
1 tablespoon snipped fresh
   parsley
1 teaspoon freeze-dried
   chives
¼ teaspoon salt*
⅛ teaspoon pepper
1⅔ cups skim milk

1 cup shredded Monterey
   Jack cheese
2 tablespoons grated
   Parmesan cheese
4 cups thinly sliced potatoes,
   ⅛ inch thick
2 cups chopped cabbage
⅓ cup thinly sliced carrot,
   ⅛ inch thick
1 teaspoon cider vinegar
¼ cup chopped unsalted
   dry roasted peanuts

4 servings

In 2-quart casserole, blend butter-flavored mix and flour. Stir in
onion, parsley, chives, salt and pepper. Blend in milk. Microwave,
uncovered, at High for 6 to 8 minutes, or until mixture thickens and
bubbles, stirring 3 times. Stir in Monterey Jack and Parmesan
cheeses, stirring until Monterey Jack cheese melts. Add potatoes,
cabbage and carrot. Stir to coat. Cover. Microwave at High for 5
minutes. Stir. Re-cover. Reduce power to 70% (Medium High).
Microwave for 15 to 20 minutes longer, or until potatoes are tender,
stirring after every 5 minutes. Let stand, covered, for 5 minutes. Stir
in vinegar. Sprinkle with peanuts before serving.

*To reduce sodium omit salt.

Per Serving:			
Calories:	372	Cholesterol:	34 mg.
Protein:	18 g.	Sodium:	900 mg.
Carbohydrate:	43 g.	Calcium:	425 mg.**
Fat:	15 g.	Exchanges:	2 starch, 1 high-fat meat, 1 vegetable, ½ skim milk, 1 fat

Basic Tomato Sauce

1 can (14½ oz.) no-salt whole
   tomatoes
1 can (6 oz.) no-salt tomato
   paste
¼ cup grated carrot
1 tablespoon finely chopped
   onion
1 clove garlic, minced
2 teaspoons olive oil
1 teaspoon packed brown
   sugar
½ teaspoon Italian seasoning

2 cups sauce

In 2-quart casserole, combine
all ingredients, stirring to break
apart tomatoes. Microwave,
uncovered, at High for 10 to 15
minutes, or until sauce boils and
flavors are blended, stirring 2 or
3 times. Serve over hot cooked
pasta or use in other recipes,
if desired.

Per Serving:	
Calories:	312
Protein:	8 g.
Carbohydrate:	50 g.
Fat:	9 g.
Cholesterol:	—
Sodium:	99 mg.
Calcium:	—
Exchanges:	10 vegetable, 1½ fat

Vegetable & Brown Rice Bake

½ cup low-fat cottage cheese
⅓ cup part-skim ricotta cheese
¼ cup buttermilk
1 teaspoon dried basil leaves
¼ teaspoon dried marjoram
    leaves
2 cups cooked brown rice,
    page 111, divided
1 medium zucchini, thinly
    sliced, divided
1 large tomato, seeded and
    chopped, divided
2 teaspoons grated Parmesan
    cheese
½ cup hot Basic Tomato Sauce,
    page 98

4 servings

In food processor or blender bowl, combine cottage cheese, ricotta cheese, buttermilk, basil and marjoram. Process until smooth. In 1-quart casserole, layer one-half the rice. Press lightly. Top with one-half the zucchini, one-half the tomato and one-half the cottage cheese mixture. Repeat layers. Sprinkle with Parmesan cheese. Cover. Microwave at 70% (Medium High) for 11 to 18 minutes, or until internal temperature in center registers 140°F, rotating dish once or twice. Let stand, covered, for 1 minute. Top each serving with 2 tablespoons Basic Tomato Sauce.

Per Serving:			
Calories:	201	Cholesterol:	9 mg.
Protein:	10 g.	Sodium:	182 mg.
Carbohydrate:	32 g.	Calcium:	118 mg.**
Fat:	4 g.	Exchanges:	1½ starch, ½ med.-fat meat, 2 vegetable

Vegetarian Stuffed Squash

3 tablespoons apple juice
2 tablespoons reduced-calorie
    margarine
¾ teaspoon ground coriander
    Dash ground cloves
2 cups cooked brown rice,
    page 111
1 pkg. (10 oz.) frozen
    black-eyed peas
1 cup frozen mixed vegetables
¾ cup unsalted sunflower nuts
¼ cup wheat germ
2 large acorn squash, about
    2½ lbs. each, cut in half

Topping:
½ cup Tangy Topper, page 27
⅛ teaspoon ground coriander

4 servings

In medium mixing bowl, combine apple juice, margarine, coriander and cloves. Cover with plastic wrap. Microwave at 70% (Medium High) for 1 to 2 minutes, or just until margarine melts. Stir. Set aside. Unwrap black-eyed peas and place on plate. Microwave at High for 2 to 4 minutes, or until defrosted. Drain. Add rice, black-eyed peas, mixed vegetables, sunflower nuts and wheat germ to apple juice mixture. Mix well. Set aside.

Remove and discard seeds from each squash half. Place cut-side down in 12 × 8-inch baking dish. Cover with plastic wrap. Microwave at High for 15 to 20 minutes, or until tender, rotating dish once. Turn cut-side up. Spoon rice mixture into squash halves. Cover with plastic wrap. Microwave at High for 5 to 8 minutes longer, or until heated through, rotating dish once. For topping, in small bowl, blend all ingredients. Spoon 2 tablespoons topping over each squash half.

Per Serving:			
Calories:	521	Cholesterol:	2 mg.
Protein:	23 g.	Sodium:	227 mg.
Carbohydrate:	62 g.	Calcium:	117 mg.**
Fat:	21 g.	Exchanges:	4 starch, 1½ high-fat meat, 1½ fat

Whole Wheat ▶ Mac-N-Cheese

1 cup uncooked whole wheat
   elbow macaroni
¼ cup chopped carrot
1 tablespoon finely chopped
   onion
1 tablespoon reduced-calorie
   margarine
2 tablespoons all-purpose flour
⅛ teaspoon dried tarragon
   leaves
   Dash pepper
1 cup buttermilk
½ cup frozen peas
1 cup shredded pasteurized
   process American cheese

4 servings

Prepare macaroni as directed
on package. Rinse with warm
water. Drain. Set aside.

In 1½-quart casserole, combine
carrot, onion and margarine.
Cover. Microwave at High for
2 to 3 minutes, or until carrot
is tender-crisp. Stir in flour,
tarragon and pepper. Blend in
buttermilk. Stir in peas. Reduce
power to 70% (Medium High).
Microwave, uncovered, for 6 to
8½ minutes, or until sauce
thickens and bubbles, stirring 2
or 3 times. Add macaroni and
American cheese. Mix well.
Microwave at 70% (Medium
High) for 2 to 3 minutes longer,
or until hot, stirring once.

Per Serving:
Calories: 280
Protein: 14 g.
Carbohydrate: 29 g.
Fat: 14 g.
Cholesterol: 32 mg.
Sodium: 259 mg.
Calcium: 289 mg.**
Exchanges: 2 starch, 1 high-fat
                 meat,1 fat

Wild Rice & Barley Dinner

4½ cups hot water, divided
½ cup uncooked medium
   pearl barley
½ cup uncooked wild rice,
   rinsed and drained
½ cup sliced fresh mushrooms
½ cup sliced carrot, ¼ inch
   thick
¼ cup sliced green onions
2 tablespoons snipped fresh
   parsley
1 clove garlic, minced
½ teaspoon bouquet garni
   seasoning
½ teaspoon low-sodium instant
   chicken bouillon granules
½ teaspoon salt*
⅛ teaspoon pepper
½ lb. fresh broccoli, cut into
   flowerets, stalk sliced
   ¼ inch thick, about
   2½ cups
1 cup frozen whole kernel
   corn
½ cup evaporated skimmed
   milk

6 servings

In 3-quart casserole, combine 1½ cups water and barley. Cover.
Microwave at High for 5 minutes. Reduce power to 50% (Medium).
Microwave for 10 minutes. Rinse and drain. Return to same
casserole. Stir in remaining 3 cups water, wild rice, mushrooms,
carrot, green onions, parsley, garlic, bouquet garni, bouillon, salt
and pepper. Re-cover. Microwave at High for 3 minutes. Reduce
power to 50% (Medium). Microwave for 45 to 55 minutes longer, or
until wild rice kernels begin to open, stirring after every 15 minutes.
Add remaining ingredients. Re-cover. Microwave at High for 8 to
11 minutes longer, or until broccoli is tender-crisp, stirring twice.

*To reduce sodium omit salt.

Per Serving:
Calories: 184   Cholesterol: 1 mg.
Protein: 8 g.   Sodium: 207 mg.
Carbohydrate: 39 g.   Calcium: 149 mg.**
Fat: 1 g.   Exchanges: 2 starch, 2 vegetable

Vegetable & Cheese Enchiladas

4 corn tortillas, 6-inch
    Vegetable oil
1 cup shredded Monterey Jack
    cheese, divided
½ cup part-skim ricotta cheese
½ teaspoon dried cilantro
    leaves
¼ teaspoon salt*
¼ teaspoon chili powder
    Dash ground cumin
1 medium tomato, seeded and
    chopped
1 cup shredded zucchini
⅓ cup finely chopped green
    pepper
¼ cup finely chopped onion
1 cup Chunky Salsa Sauce,
    page 26, divided

4 servings

*To reduce sodium omit salt.

Per Serving:	
Calories:	238
Protein:	13 g.
Carbohydrate:	19 g.
Fat:	12 g.
Cholesterol:	39 mg.
Sodium:	358 mg.
Calcium:	310 mg.**
Exchanges:	1 starch, 1 high-fat meat, 1 vegetable, 1 fat

How to Microwave Vegetable & Cheese Enchiladas

Prepare tortillas as directed on package for enchiladas. Set aside. In small mixing bowl, blend ½ cup Monterey Jack cheese, ricotta cheese, cilantro, salt, chili powder and cumin. Set aside.

Combine tomato, zucchini, green pepper and onion in 1-quart casserole. Cover. Microwave at High for 4 to 6 minutes, or until onion is tender-crisp, stirring once.

Let stand, covered, for 3 minutes. Drain. Press to remove excess moisture. Add ½ cup Chunky Salsa Sauce to vegetables. Mix well. Set aside.

Spread about ¼ cup cheese mixture on a tortilla. Spread about ⅓ cup vegetable mixture down center of tortilla. Roll tortilla around filling.

Arrange seam-side down in 9-inch square baking dish. Repeat with remaining tortillas and filling. Pour ½ cup Chunky Salsa Sauce over enchiladas. Cover with wax paper.

Microwave at High for 4 minutes, rotating dish once. Sprinkle with ½ cup Monterey Jack cheese. Microwave, uncovered, at High for 1½ to 2½ minutes longer, or until cheese melts.

Pita with Falafel Filling ▼

Falafel Filling:
½ cup chopped onion
¼ cup snipped fresh parsley
2 tablespoons sesame seed
1 tablespoon vegetable oil
½ teaspoon dried oregano
    leaves
½ teaspoon dried mint leaves
½ teaspoon paprika
⅛ teaspoon garlic powder
⅛ teaspoon ground allspice
⅛ teaspoon cayenne
1 can (15 oz.) garbanzo beans,
    rinsed and drained

½ cup low-fat plain yogurt
2 tablespoons wheat germ

4 servings

For one sandwich:
1 whole wheat pita bread,
    6-inch, cut in half
2 tablespoons shredded
    Muenster cheese, divided
½ cup shredded lettuce,
    divided
2 slices tomato, divided
½ cup alfalfa sprouts, divided
2 tablespoons chopped green
    pepper, divided

1 serving

In 1-quart casserole, combine onion, parsley, sesame, vegetable oil, oregano, mint, paprika, garlic powder, allspice and cayenne. Mix well. Cover. Microwave at High for 3 to 4 minutes, or until onion is tender-crisp, stirring once. Cool slightly. Place in food processor or blender bowl. Add remaining filling ingredients. Process until smooth.

Spoon 3 tablespoons filling and 1 tablespoon Muenster cheese into each pita half. Place on paper plate. Microwave at High for 45 seconds to 1 minute, or until cheese melts. Fill each pita half with ¼ cup lettuce, 1 tablespoon green pepper, 1 slice tomato and ¼ cup alfalfa sprouts. Remaining filling can be refrigerated, covered, for up to 3 days.

Per Serving:			
Calories:	349	Cholesterol:	15 mg.
Protein:	18 g.	Sodium:	460 mg.
Carbohydrate:	41 g.	Calcium:	192 mg.**
Fat:	13 g.	Exchanges:	2½ starch, 1½ high-fat meat, 1 vegetable

Stuffed Tostadas

1 can (16 oz.) refried beans
1 can (14½ oz.) no-salt whole
    tomatoes, drained and
    chopped, divided
2 tablespoons canned
    chopped green chilies
½ teaspoon ground cumin
¼ teaspoon dried oregano
    leaves
⅛ teaspoon garlic powder
4 flour tortillas, 8-inch
1 cup shredded Cheddar
    cheese
2 cups shredded lettuce
¼ cup sliced green onions

4 servings

In 1½-quart casserole, combine beans, one-half the tomatoes, the chilies, cumin, oregano and garlic powder. Mix well. Microwave at High for 5½ to 6½ minutes, or until heated through and bubbly around edges, stirring after every 2 minutes. Place one tortilla on each of two large plates. Top each tortilla with one-half the bean mixture. Sprinkle each with ¼ cup Cheddar cheese. Top each with another tortilla and ¼ cup cheese. Microwave, one at a time, at 70% (Medium High) for 1 to 2 minutes, or until cheese melts. Top each tostada with 1 cup lettuce, 2 tablespoons green onion and one-half the remaining tomatoes. Top each tostada with 1 tablespoon Tangy Topper, page 27, and 1 table-spoon Chunky Salsa Sauce, page 26, if desired. Cut each tostada in half to serve.

Per Serving:	
Calories:	365
Protein:	15 g.
Carbohydrate:	47 g.
Fat:	11 g.
Cholesterol:	49 mg.
Sodium:	783 mg.
Calcium:	243 mg.**
Exchanges:	3 starch, 1 high-fat meat, ½ vegetable

Spaghetti with ▶ Mushroom Sauce

8 oz. uncooked whole wheat
   spaghetti
1 can (14½ oz.) no-salt whole
   tomatoes
12 oz. fresh mushrooms, thinly
   sliced
1 can (6 oz.) no-salt tomato
   paste
¼ cup grated carrot
2 tablespoons finely chopped
   onion
2 tablespoons red wine
1 tablespoon olive oil
1 teaspoon sugar
½ teaspoon Italian seasoning
¼ teaspoon salt*
½ cup grated Parmesan
   cheese

4 servings, 1 cup sauce each

Prepare spaghetti as directed
on package. Rinse with warm
water. Drain. Set aside. In
2-quart casserole, combine all
ingredients, except spaghetti
and Parmesan cheese. Cover.
Microwave at High for 10 to 17
minutes, or until mushrooms are
tender and flavors are blended,
stirring after every 5 minutes.
Place spaghetti on platter. Pour
sauce over spaghetti. Sprinkle
with Parmesan cheese.

*To reduce sodium omit salt.

Per Serving:	
Calories:	355
Protein:	16 g.
Carbohydrate:	57 g.
Fat:	8 g.
Cholesterol:	10 mg.
Sodium:	392 mg.
Calcium:	191 mg.**
Exchanges:	3 starch, 2 vegetable, ½ med.-fat meat, 1 fat

Spinach Manicotti

8 manicotti shells
Filling:
2 pkgs. (10 oz. each) frozen
   chopped spinach
1 cup low-fat cottage cheese
¼ cup finely chopped onion
2 tablespoons grated
   Parmesan cheese
½ teaspoon dried basil leaves
¼ teaspoon dried oregano
   leaves

⅛ teaspoon garlic powder
⅛ teaspoon pepper

Sauce:
1 cup skim milk
2 teaspoons all-purpose flour
1 tablespoon snipped fresh
   parsley
½ cup low-moisture, part-skim
   mozzarella cheese
2 tablespoons grated
   Parmesan cheese

4 servings

Prepare manicotti as directed on package. Rinse with cold water.
Drain. Cover with plastic wrap. Set aside. Unwrap spinach and
place on plate. Microwave at High for 6 to 8 minutes, or until
defrosted, rotating plate once. Drain. Press to remove excess
moisture. In medium mixing bowl, combine spinach and remaining
filling ingredients. Mix well. Stuff each manicotti shell with about ⅓
cup filling. Arrange in 10-inch square baking dish. Set aside.

For sauce, in small mixing bowl, blend milk and flour. Stir in
parsley. Microwave at High for 2 to 4 minutes, or until sauce
thickens, stirring after first 2 minutes, then after every minute. Add
mozzarella and Parmesan cheeses. Stir until mozzarella cheese
melts. Pour evenly over manicotti. Cover with wax paper. Microwave at 70% (Medium High) for 9 to 14 minutes longer, or until
internal temperature registers 145°F, rotating dish once or twice.
Let stand, covered, for 1 minute.

Per Serving:			
Calories:	323	Cholesterol:	15 mg.
Protein:	24 g.	Sodium:	521 mg.
Carbohydrate:	46 g.	Calcium:	447 mg.**
Fat:	6 g.	Exchanges:	2 starch, 1½ lean meat, 2 vegetable, ½ skim milk

Vegetables, Pasta & Grains

Vegetable Chart

Type	Amount	Microwave Time at High	Procedure
Artichokes, fresh	2 med. 4 med.	5½ to 8½ min. 9½ to 15 min.	Trim stems. Cut 1 inch from tops. Trim sharp ends from each leaf. Rinse and shake off excess water. Brush with lemon juice to prevent browning. Wrap each with plastic wrap. Rearrange once. Let stand 3 minutes.
Hearts, frozen	9-oz. pkg.	6 to 8 min.	1-qt. casserole with 2 tablespoons water. Cover. Stir once. Let stand 3 minutes.
Asparagus, fresh	1 lb.	7 to 10 min.	Trim tough ends. 10-in. square casserole. Place tips to center. Add ¼ cup water. Cover. Rearrange once. Let stand 3 minutes.
frozen	10-oz. pkg.	7 to 9 min.	1-qt. casserole with 2 tablespoons water. Cover. Rearrange once. Let stand 3 minutes.
Beans, Green or Wax, fresh	1 lb.	12½ to 17½ min.	Trim ends. Cut into 1½-in. pieces. 1½-qt. casserole with ½ cup water. Cover. Stir once. Let stand 5 minutes.
Green, Wax or Lima, frozen	9-oz. pkg.	5 to 8 min.	1-qt. casserole with 2 tablespoons water. Cover. Stir once. Let stand 3 minutes.
Broccoli, Spears, fresh	1 lb.	8 to 12 min.	Trim tough stalk. Cut into spears. 10-in. square casserole. Place flowerettes to center. Add ¼ cup water. Cover. Rearrange once. Let stand 3 minutes.
frozen	10-oz. pkg.	7 to 10 min.	1-qt. casserole with 2 tablespoons water. Cover. Stir once. Let stand 3 minutes.
Brussels Sprouts, fresh	1 lb.	4 to 8 min.	Cut "X" in bottom of each sprout. 1½-qt. casserole with ¼ cup water. Cover. Stir once. Let stand 3 minutes.
frozen	1 lb.	6 to 8 min.	1-qt. casserole with 2 tablespoons water. Cover. Stir once. Let stand 3 minutes.
Cabbage, Shredded, fresh	¾ lb. (4 cups)	6 to 9 min.	1-qt. casserole with ¼ cup water. Cover. Stir once. Let stand 3 minutes.
Wedges, fresh	1 med. head (about 1½ lbs.)	12 to 19 min.	Cut into 4 wedges. 10-in. square casserole with ¼ cup water. Cover. Rotate dish once. Let stand 3 minutes.
Carrots, Sliced, fresh	2 cups sliced (⅛ in. thick)	4 to 8 min.	1-qt. casserole with 2 tablespoons water. Cover. Stir once. Let stand 3 minutes.
frozen	2 cups	6 to 8 min.	1-qt. casserole with 2 tablespoons water. Cover. Stir once. Let stand 3 minutes.
Baby, frozen	2 cups	5 to 7 min.	1-qt. casserole with 2 tablespoons water. Cover. Stir once. Let stand 3 minutes.
Cauliflower, Whole, fresh	1 med. (about 2 lbs.)	7½ to 14 min.	Remove leaf and stem. Rinse. Place core-side-up on platter. Cover with plastic wrap. Turn over after ½ time. Let stand 5 minutes.

Type	Amount	Microwave Time at High	Procedure
Cauliflower, Continued			
Flowerets, fresh	1 med. (about 2 lbs.) (5 cups)	7 to 10 min.	1½-qt. casserole with ¼ cup water. Cover. Stir once. Let stand 5 minutes.
frozen	10-oz. pkg.	5 to 8 min.	1-qt. casserole with 2 tablespoons water. Cover. Stir once. Let stand 3 minutes.
Corn,			
on Cob, fresh	2 med. ears 4 med. ears	5 to 10 min. 8 to 16 min.	Remove husk. 10-in. square casserole with 2 tablespoons water. Cover. Rearrange once. Let stand 5 minutes.
frozen	2 small ears 4 small ears	3 to 7 min. 5 to 10 min.	9-in. square baking dish with 2 tablespoons water. Cover. Rearrange once. Let stand 5 minutes.
Whole Kernel, frozen	10-oz. pkg.	5 to 7 min.	1-qt. casserole with 2 tablespoons water. Cover. Stir once. Let stand 3 minutes.
Peas,			
Black-eyed, frozen	10-oz. pkg.	8 to 9 min.	1-qt. casserole with ¼ cup water. Cover. Stir once. Let stand 3 minutes.
Green, fresh	2 cups (about 2 lbs.)	4 to 6 min.	Shell peas. 1-qt. casserole with ¼ cup water. Cover. Stir once. Let stand 3 minutes.
frozen	10-oz. pkg.	6 to 8 min.	1-qt. casserole with 2 tablespoons water. Cover. Stir once. Let stand 2 minutes.
Potatoes,			
Baking	2 med. 4 med.	6½ to 8 min. 10 to 14 min.	Pierce. Arrange in circle on paper towel in oven. Rearrange once. Let stand, wrapped in foil, 5 to 10 minutes.
New	1 lb. (2-in. dia.)	8 to 10 min.	Peel. Cut large potatoes. 1½-qt. casserole with ¼ cup water. Cover. Stir once. Let stand 5 minutes.
Spinach,			
fresh	1 lb.	6 to 9 min.	Wash. 2-qt. casserole with ¼ cup water. Cover. Stir once. Let stand 3 minutes.
frozen	10-oz. pkg.	5 to 8 min.	1-qt. casserole with 2 tablespoons water. Cover. Stir once. Let stand 3 minutes.
Squash,			
Acorn, fresh	1 whole 2 whole	8½ to 11 min. 13 to 16 min.	Cut in halves. Remove seeds. 9 or 10-in. baking dish with ¼ cup water. Cover with plastic wrap. Rearrange once. Let stand 5 minutes.
Mashed, frozen	10-oz. pkg.	6 to 8 min.	1-qt. casserole with no water. Cover. Stir once. Let stand 3 minutes.
Zucchini, Sliced, fresh	2 cups	3½ to 5½ min.	1-qt. casserole with 2 tablespoons water. Cover. Stir twice. Let stand 3 minutes.
Sweet Potatoes	2 small 4 small	5 to 9 min. 8 to 13 min.	Pierce. Arrange in circle on paper towel in oven. Rearrange once. Let stand, wrapped in foil, 5 to 10 minutes.

Dried Beans & Peas Chart

Type	Ingredients	Microwave Time	Procedure
Black Beans or Turtle Beans (1 lb.)	6 cups hot water 1 medium onion, chopped 1 bay leaf	High 10 min., 50% (Med.) 1½ to 2 hours	Sort, rinse and drain beans. Combine beans and remaining ingredients in 5-qt. casserole. Cover. Microwave as directed, or until tender, stirring twice. Let stand, covered, 10 to 20 minutes.
Garbanzo Beans or Chick Peas (1 lb.)	6 cups hot water 1 medium onion, chopped 1 bay leaf	High 10 min., 50% (Med.) 1¾ to 2¼ hours	Sort, rinse and drain beans. Combine beans and remaining ingredients in 5-qt. casserole. Cover. Microwave as directed, or until tender, stirring twice. Let stand, covered, 10 to 20 minutes.
Kidney or Red Beans (1 lb.)	6 cups hot water 1 medium onion, chopped 1 bay leaf	High 10 min., 50% (Med.) 1¾ to 2¼ hours	Sort, rinse and drain beans. Combine beans and remaining ingredients in 5-qt. casserole. Cover. Microwave as directed, or until tender, stirring 3 times. Let stand, covered, 10 to 20 minutes.
Lentils (1 lb.)	6 cups hot water 2 cloves garlic, halved 1 bay leaf	High 10 min., 50% (med.) 30 min. to 1 hour	Sort, rinse and drain lentils. Combine lentils and remaining ingredients in 5-qt. casserole. Cover. Microwave as directed, or until tender, stirring once. Let stand, covered, 5 to 10 minutes.
Navy Beans (1 lb.)	6 cups hot water 1 medium onion, chopped 1 bay leaf	High 10 min., 50% (Med.) 1¾ to 2¼ hours	Sort, rinse and drain beans. Combine beans and remaining ingredients in 5-qt. casserole. Cover. Microwave as directed, or until tender, stirring 3 times. Let stand, covered, 10 to 20 minutes.
Northern Beans (1 lb.)	6 cups hot water 1 medium onion, chopped 1 bay leaf	High 10 min., 50% (Med.) 1½ to 2 hours	Sort, rinse and drain beans. Combine beans and remaining ingredients in 5-qt. casserole. Cover. Microwave as directed, or until tender, stirring twice. Let stand, covered, 10 to 20 minutes.
Pinto Beans (1 lb.)	6 cups hot water 1 medium onion, chopped 1 bay leaf	High 10 min., 50% (Med.) 1½ to 2 hours	Sort, rinse and drain beans. Combine beans and remaining ingredients in 5-qt. casserole. Cover. Microwave as directed, or until tender, stirring twice. Let stand, covered, 10 to 20 minutes.
Split Peas (1 lb.)	6 cups hot water 1 medium onion, chopped ¼ teaspoon peppercorn	High 10 min., 50% (Med.) 30 min. to 1 hour	Sort, rinse and drain peas. Combine peas and remaining ingredients in 5-qt. casserole. Cover. Microwave as directed, or until tender, stirring once. Let stand, covered, 5 to 10 minutes.

Rice & Grains Chart

Type	Amount	Utensil	Hot Water	Microwave Time at High	Procedure
Bulgur	1 cup	Med. mixing bowl	3 cups	5½ to 9 min.	Microwave water until boiling. Stir in bulgur. Let stand 30 minutes. Drain. Press to remove excess moisture.
Couscous	⅔ cup	1-qt. casserole	⅔ cup	2 to 3½ min.	Combine ingredients. Cover. Microwave until liquid is absorbed and couscous is tender. Let stand, covered, 3 to 5 minutes.
Cream of Wheat® Regular	2½ Tbls. 1-qt. casserole ⅓ cup ⅔ cup	1-qt. casserole 2-qt. casserole 3-qt. casserole	1¼ cups 1¾ cups 3½ cups	4 to 6 min. 6 to 8 min 9 to 12 min.	Combine ingredients. Microwave, uncovered, until cereal is desired consistency, stirring 2 or 3 times.
Quick-cooking	2½ Tbls. ⅓ cup ⅔ cup	1-qt. casserole 2-qt. casserole 3-qt. casserole	¾ cup 1⅓ cups 2¾ cups	1½ to 3 min. 2½ to 4 min. 5 to 6½ min.	Combine ingredients. Microwave, uncovered, until cereal is desired consistency, stirring 2 or 3 times.
Grits, Quick-cooking	3 Tbls. ½ cup ¾ cup	1-qt. casserole 2-qt. casserole 3-qt. casserole	¾ cup 1½ cups 2¾ cups	2½ to 3 min. 3 to 3½ min. 6 to 8 min.	Combine ingredients. Microwave, uncovered, until grits are desired consistency, stirring 2 or 3 times.
Oats, Old-fashioned	⅓ cup ⅔ cup 1⅓ cups	1-qt. casserole 1½-qt. casserole 2-qt. casserole	¾ cup 1⅓ cups 2½ cups	4 to 6 min. 5 to 7 min. 7 to 10 min.	Combine ingredients. Microwave, uncovered, until cereal is desired consistency, stirring 2 or 3 times.
Quick-cooking	⅓ cup ⅔ cup 1⅓ cups	1-qt. casserole 1½-qt. casserole 2-qt. casserole	¾ cup 1½ cups 3 cups	2 to 4 min. 4 to 6 min. 6 to 8 min.	Combine ingredients. Microwave, uncovered, until cereal is desired consistency, stirring 2 or 3 times.
Rice, Long-grain Converted	1 cup	2-qt. casserole	2¼ cups	High 5 min., 50% (Med.) 15 to 22 min.	Combine ingredients. Cover. Microwave until liquid is absorbed and rice is tender. Let stand, covered, 5 minutes.
Long-grain White	1 cup	2-qt. casserole	2 cups	High 5 min., 50% (Med.) 12 to 15 min.	Combine ingredients. Cover. Microwave until liquid is absorbed and rice is tender. Let stand, covered, 5 minutes.
Brown	1¼ cups	3-qt. casserole	2⅓ cups	High 5 min., 50% (Med.) 35 to 45 min.	Combine ingredients. Cover. Microwave until liquid is absorbed and rice is tender. Let stand, covered, 5 minutes.
Wild	1 cup	3-qt. casserole	2¾ cups	High 5 min., 50% (Med.) 20 to 30 min.	Rinse rice. Drain. Combine ingredients. Cover. Microwave until rice is tender and kernels begin to open. Drain.

Vegetables

◄ Artichokes with Dips

4 artichokes (10 to 12 oz. each)
¼ cup ready-to-serve
    low-sodium chicken broth
2 tablespoons lemon juice

Onion Mustard Dip: (Pictured)

2 teaspoons finely chopped
    onion
1 clove garlic, minced
1 teaspoon lemon juice
¼ cup low-fat plain yogurt

¼ cup low-calorie mayonnaise
2 teaspoons Dijon mustard

Buttery Dill Dip:

¼ cup reconstituted natural
    butter-flavored mix
1 teaspoon lime juice
1 teaspoon snipped fresh
    parsley
⅛ teaspoon dried dill weed
3 to 4 drops hot pepper sauce

4 servings

Trim stems close to base of each artichoke. Cut 1 inch off tops and trim sharp ends off each artichoke leaf. Rinse and shake off excess water. Place artichokes upright in 9-inch square baking dish. Pour broth and lemon juice over artichokes. Cover with plastic wrap. Microwave at High for 16 to 22 minutes, or until base is tender and bottom leaf pulls out easily, rearranging and basting with juices twice. Let stand, covered, for 5 minutes. Serve with choice of dips.

For Onion Mustard Dip, in 1-cup measure, combine onion, garlic and lemon juice. Cover with plastic wrap. Microwave at High for 30 seconds to 1 minute, or until onion is tender. Stir in remaining ingredients.

For Buttery Dill Dip, in 1-cup measure, combine all ingredients. Mix well. Microwave at High for 30 seconds to 1 minute, or until heated. Stir before serving.

Onion Mustard Dip			
Per Serving:			
Calories:	116	Cholesterol:	6 mg.
Protein:	2 g.	Sodium:	90 mg.
Carbohydrate:	18 g.	Calcium:	—
Fat:	8 g.	Exchanges:	3 vegetable, 1 fat

Buttery Dill Dip			
Per Serving:			
Calories:	72	Cholesterol:	—
Protein:	2 g.	Sodium:	164 mg.
Carbohydrate:	17 g.	Calcium:	—
Fat:	—	Exchanges:	3 vegetable

Herbed Artichokes & Potatoes

3 tablespoons reconstituted
    natural butter-flavored mix
1 teaspoon lemon juice
¼ teaspoon dried rosemary
    leaves, crushed
⅛ teaspoon garlic powder
    Dash pepper
8 oz. new potatoes, about
    1½ inches
1 pkg. (9 oz.) frozen artichoke
    hearts

6 servings

In 1-quart casserole, combine butter-flavored mix, lemon juice, rosemary, garlic powder and pepper. Cover. Microwave at High for 30 seconds to 1 minute, or until very hot. Remove thin strip of peel around center of potato. Add potatoes. Stir. Re-cover. Microwave at High for 4 minutes. Add artichoke hearts. Re-cover. Microwave at High for 6 to 10 minutes longer, or until artichokes are hot and potatoes are tender, stirring once. Let stand, covered, for 2 minutes.

Per Serving:	
Calories:	138
Protein:	4 g.
Carbohydrate:	32 g.
Fat:	—
Cholesterol:	—
Sodium:	65 mg.
Calcium:	—
Exchanges:	2 starch

Asparagus à la Orange ▲

1 lb. fresh asparagus, trimmed
¼ cup orange juice
1 tablespoon reconstituted
   natural butter-flavored mix
1 teaspoon cornstarch
¼ teaspoon dried marjoram
   leaves
1 medium orange, sectioned

4 servings

Arrange asparagus with tender ends toward center of 9-inch round baking dish. Set aside. In 1-cup measure, combine remaining ingredients, except orange sections. Pour over asparagus. Cover with plastic wrap. Microwave at High for 5 to 7 minutes, or until tender, rearranging asparagus and stirring sauce after half the time. Top with orange sections. Let stand, covered, for 3 minutes.

Per Serving:
Calories: 40
Protein: 2 g.
Carbohydrate: 9 g.
Fat: —
Cholesterol: —
Sodium: 29 mg.
Calcium: —
Exchanges: 2 vegetable

Sunchoke Sauté

1 lb. Jerusalem artichokes,
   trimmed and sliced ¼ inch
   thick
¼ cup reconstituted natural
   butter-flavored mix
2 teaspoons red wine vinegar
1 tablespoon snipped fresh
   parsley
½ teaspoon dry mustard
½ teaspoon grated lemon peel
⅛ teaspoon pepper
1 tablespoon unsalted
   sunflower nuts

4 servings

In 2-quart casserole, combine all ingredients, except nuts. Mix well. Cover. Microwave at High for 8 to 12 minutes, or until tender, stirring after half the time. Sprinkle with sunflower nuts.

Per Serving:
Calories: 77
Protein: 2 g.
Carbohydrate: 15 g.
Fat: 1 g.
Cholesterol: —
Sodium: 105 mg.
Calcium: —
Exchanges: 1 starch

Smoky Baked Beans

2 cans (16 oz. each) Great
   Northern beans
1 can (8 oz.) no-salt tomato
   sauce
¼ cup chopped onion
2 tablespoons light molasses
2 teaspoons prepared mustard
¼ teaspoon liquid smoke

6 servings

In 1-quart casserole, combine all ingredients. Mix well. Cover with wax paper. Microwave at High for 15 to 20 minutes, or until onion is tender and flavors are blended, stirring once.

Per Serving:
Calories: 102
Protein: 4 g.
Carbohydrate: 21 g.
Fat: 1 g.
Cholesterol: —
Sodium: 197 mg.
Calcium: —
Exchanges: 1½ starch

French Green Beans ▲ & Pears

2 tablespoons chopped pecans
1 tablespoon reduced-calorie
    margarine
1 pkg. (10 oz.) frozen
    French-style green beans
¼ teaspoon dried summer
    savory leaves
1 can (8½ oz.) unsweetened
    pear slices, drained

4 servings

In 1½-quart casserole, combine
pecans and margarine. Microwave at High for 1½ to 2
minutes, or until margarine
melts. Add beans and summer
savory. Re-cover. Microwave at
High for 4 minutes. Stir to break
apart beans. Add pears.
Re-cover. Microwave at High
for 2 to 3 minutes longer, or
until beans are tender.

Per Serving:	
Calories:	83
Protein:	1 g.
Carbohydrate:	12 g.
Fat:	6 g.
Cholesterol:	—
Sodium:	29 mg.
Calcium:	—
Exchanges:	1 vegetable, ½ fruit, 1 fat

Mexican Bean Bake

¼ cup chopped onion
¼ cup chopped green pepper
1 clove garlic, minced
1 can (8 oz.) no-salt tomato
    sauce
1½ teaspoons chili powder
¼ teaspoon sugar
    Dash ground cumin
1 can (16 oz.) pinto beans,
    rinsed and drained
1 medium tomato, seeded
    and chopped

4 servings

In 1-quart casserole, combine all
ingredients, except beans and
tomato. Mix well. Microwave at
High for 5 to 10 minutes, or until
peppers are tender and flavors
are blended, stirring once or
twice. Add beans and tomato.
Stir. Microwave at High for 3 to
5 minutes longer, or until hot
and bubbly, stirring once.

Per Serving:	
Calories:	117
Protein:	6 g.
Carbohydrate:	22 g.
Fat:	2 g.
Cholesterol:	—
Sodium:	290 mg.
Calcium:	—
Exchanges:	1½ starch

Hot Triple Bean Salad

1 pkg. (10 oz.) frozen cut
    green beans
½ cup thinly sliced onion
1 clove garlic, minced
⅓ cup reduced-calorie Italian
    dressing
1 can (16 oz.) pinto beans,
    rinsed and drained
1 can (15½ oz.) butter beans,
    rinsed and drained

8 servings

In 2-quart casserole, combine
green beans, onion, garlic and
Italian dressing. Cover. Microwave at High for 6 to 8 minutes,
or until onion is tender, stirring
to break apart beans after half
the time. Add remaining ingredients. Re-cover. Microwave at
High for 3 to 6 minutes longer,
or until salad is hot.

Per Serving:	
Calories:	68
Protein:	3 g.
Carbohydrate:	12 g.
Fat:	2 g.
Cholesterol:	—
Sodium:	517 mg.
Calcium:	—
Exchanges:	½ starch, 1 vegetable

Beets with Horseradish Sauce ▲

1 small onion, thinly sliced,
　　separated into rings
1 teaspoon lemon juice
　　Dash pepper
1 can (16 oz.) no-salt diced
　　beets, drained
　　(reserve liquid)
1 tablespoon beet liquid

Horseradish Sauce:
¼ cup Tangy Topper, page 27
1 teaspoon snipped fresh
　　parsley
1 teaspoon cream-style
　　horseradish
　　Dash dried dill weed

4 servings

In 1-quart casserole, combine onion, lemon juice and pepper.
Cover. Microwave at High for 2 to 4 minutes, or until onion is
tender, stirring once. Stir in beets and 1 tablespoon beet liquid.
Re-cover. Microwave at High for 2 to 4 minutes, or until heated
through. In small bowl, combine all sauce ingredients. Mix well.
Spoon over each serving.

Per Serving:			
Calories:	44	Cholesterol:	4 mg.
Protein:	3 g.	Sodium:	85 mg.
Carbohydrate:	7 g.	Calcium:	28 mg.
Fat:	—	Exchanges:	1½ vegetable

Creamy Broccoli & Beans

2 tablespoons reduced-calorie
　　margarine
2 tablespoons finely chopped
　　onion
¼ teaspoon Italian seasoning
1 teaspoon all-purpose flour
3 tablespoons skim milk
½ lb. fresh broccoli, cut-up,
　　about 2 cups
1 can (16 oz.) wax beans,
　　rinsed and drained
1 tablespoon grated Parmesan
　　cheese

4 servings

In 1½-quart casserole, combine
margarine, onion and Italian
seasoning. Microwave at High
for 2 to 2½ minutes, or until
onion is tender. Stir in flour.
Blend in milk. Add broccoli and
beans. Stir. Cover. Microwave at
High for 5 to 6 minutes longer,
or until broccoli is tender and
sauce thickens slightly. Sprinkle
with Parmesan cheese.

Per Serving:	
Calories:	88
Protein:	5 g.
Carbohydrate:	10 g.
Fat:	8 g.
Cholesterol:	1 mg.
Sodium:	389 mg.
Calcium:	152 mg.**
Exchanges:	2 vegetable, 1½ fat

Mediterranean Broccoli ▶ & Carrot

1½ cups water
⅓ cup bulgur or cracked wheat
½ lb. fresh broccoli, cut into flowerets, about 2 cups
½ cup chopped carrot
¼ cup sliced green onions
1 tablespoon reduced-calorie margarine
¼ teaspoon curry powder
1 tablespoon unsalted sunflower nuts

4 servings

Place water in 2-cup measure. Microwave at High for 2 to 5 minutes, or until water boils. Place bulgur in small mixing bowl. Add boiling water. Cover and let stand for 30 minutes to soften. Drain and press out excess moisture. Set aside.

In 1½-quart casserole, combine all ingredients, except bulgur and nuts. Mix well. Cover. Microwave at High for 5 to 8 minutes, or until vegetables are tender, stirring twice. Stir in bulgur and sunflower nuts. Re-cover. Microwave at High for 2 minutes longer, or until heated through.

Per Serving:	
Calories:	135
Protein:	4 g.
Carbohydrate:	20 g.
Fat:	5 g.
Cholesterol:	—
Sodium:	42 mg.
Calcium:	97 mg.**
Exchanges:	1 starch, 1 vegetable, 1 fat

Brussels Sprouts & Herb Cheese Sauce

1 lb. fresh Brussels sprouts, trimmed and cut in half lengthwise
¼ cup water

Herb Cheese Sauce:
1 tablespoon all-purpose flour
½ teaspoon dried chervil leaves
¼ teaspoon onion powder
⅛ teaspoon dried basil leaves
⅛ teaspoon salt*
Dash pepper
¾ cup skim milk
1 tablespoon reconstituted natural butter-flavored mix
¼ cup shredded Swiss cheese

6 servings

In 1-quart casserole, combine Brussels sprouts and water. Cover. Microwave at High for 5 to 8 minutes, or until tender-crisp, stirring once or twice. Drain. Let stand, covered, while preparing sauce.

In 4-cup measure, combine flour, chervil, onion powder, basil, salt and pepper. Blend in milk and butter-flavored mix. Microwave at High for 2¾ to 4½ minutes, or until sauce thickens and bubbles, stirring 2 or 3 times. Stir in Swiss cheese until cheese melts. Pour sauce over Brussels sprouts.

*To reduce sodium omit salt.

Per Serving:				
Calories:	55	Cholesterol:	1 mg.	
Protein:	4 g.	Sodium:	77 mg.	
Carbohydrate:	11 g.	Calcium:	77 mg.**	
Fat:	—	Exchanges:	2 vegetable	

Steamed Cabbage

¾ cup light beer
¼ teaspoon caraway seed,
   crushed
¼ teaspoon salt*
   Dash dried dill weed
1 head cabbage, about 1¾ lbs.,
   cored and cut into
   4 wedges

4 servings

In 2-quart casserole, combine
beer, caraway, salt and dill.
Cover. Microwave at High for
1 to 2 minutes, or until hot. Add
cabbage. Re-cover. Microwave
at High for 12 to 21 minutes
longer, or until tender-crisp,
rotating dish once. Let stand,
covered, for 3 minutes.

*To reduce sodium omit salt.

Per Serving:	
Calories:	27
Protein:	1 g.
Carbohydrate:	5 g.
Fat:	—
Cholesterol:	—
Sodium:	134 mg.
Calcium:	—
Exchanges:	1 vegetable

Spiced Red Cabbage ▲

2 tablespoons apple juice
1 tablespoon packed brown
   sugar
2 teaspoons cider vinegar
¼ teaspoon salt*
⅛ teaspoon ground cinnamon
   Dash ground cloves
4 cups shredded red cabbage
½ cup chopped apple
¼ cup chopped onion
1 tablespoon reduced-calorie
   margarine

4 servings

In 2-quart casserole, blend
apple juice, sugar, vinegar, salt,
cinnamon and cloves. Add
remaining ingredients. Mix well.
Cover. Microwave at High for
8 to 12 minutes, or until tender-
crisp, stirring twice. Let stand,
covered, for 3 minutes.

*To reduce sodium omit salt.

Per Serving:	
Calories:	91
Protein:	1 g.
Carbohydrate:	13 g.
Fat:	4 g.
Cholesterol:	—
Sodium:	163 mg.
Calcium:	—
Exchanges:	2½ vegetable, ½ fat

Cabbage & Linguine

2 oz. uncooked linguine
1 tablespoon reduced-calorie
   margarine
1 teaspoon all-purpose flour
¼ teaspoon ground mace
¼ cup skim milk
4 cups shredded cabbage
1 tablespoon snipped fresh
   parsley

4 servings

Prepare linguine as directed
on package. Rinse with warm
water. Drain and place in
medium mixing bowl. Set aside.

Place margarine in 2-quart
casserole. Microwave at 70%
(Medium High) for 20 to 30
seconds, or until margarine
melts. Stir in flour and mace.
Blend in milk. Add cabbage
and parsley. Mix well. Cover.
Microwave at High for 6 to
11 minutes, or until cabbage
is tender-crisp, stirring after half
the time. Add linguine.
Toss lightly.

Per Serving:	
Calories:	89
Protein:	3 g.
Carbohydrate:	15 g.
Fat:	4 g.
Cholesterol:	—
Sodium:	53 mg.
Calcium:	69 mg.
Exchanges:	½ starch, 1 vegetable, ½ fat

Autumn Carrots

2 cups shredded carrots
1 medium apple, cored and
   coarsely chopped
2 tablespoons reconstituted
   natural butter-flavored mix
1 tablespoon chopped almonds
½ teaspoon ground coriander

4 servings

In 1-quart casserole, combine
all ingredients. Mix well. Cover.
Microwave at High for 5 to 8
minutes, or until carrots are
tender-crisp, stirring once. Let
stand, covered, for 1 minute.

Per Serving:	
Calories:	58
Protein:	1 g.
Carbohydrate:	12 g.
Fat:	1 g.
Cholesterol:	—
Sodium:	72 mg.
Calcium:	—
Exchanges:	2 vegetable

Herb-steamed Cauliflower

½ cup ready-to-serve
   low-sodium chicken broth
½ teaspoon dried thyme leaves
¼ teaspoon dried marjoram
   leaves
1 bay leaf
1 medium head cauliflower,
   about 1½ lbs., trimmed

4 servings

In 3-quart casserole, combine chicken broth, thyme, marjoram and bay leaf. Place cauliflower in casserole upside down. Cover. Microwave at High for 13 to 20 minutes, or until base is tender, turning cauliflower over after half the time. Let stand, covered, for 5 minutes. Remove bay leaf.

Per Serving:	
Calories:	26
Protein:	2 g.
Carbohydrate:	5 g.
Fat:	—
Cholesterol:	—
Sodium:	14 mg.
Calcium:	—
Exchanges:	1 vegetable

Cauliflower & Mushrooms with Yogurt Sauce

2 cups frozen cauliflowerets
2 tablespoons chopped onion
2 tablespoons water
1 tablespoon snipped fresh
   parsley
¼ teaspoon dried marjoram
   leaves

1 cup sliced fresh mushrooms

Yogurt Sauce:
⅓ cup low-fat plain yogurt
⅛ teaspoon salt*
   Dash pepper

4 servings

In 1-quart casserole, combine cauliflowerets, onion, water, parsley and marjoram. Cover. Microwave at High for 4 minutes. Stir in mushrooms. Re-cover. Microwave at High for 2 to 4 minutes longer, or until vegetables are tender-crisp. Drain. Let stand, covered, while preparing sauce.

In 1-cup measure, blend all sauce ingredients. Microwave at 50% (Medium) for 30 seconds to 1 minute, or until heated through. Pour over vegetables.

*To reduce sodium omit salt.

Per Serving:			
Calories:	31	Cholesterol:	1 mg.
Protein:	3 g.	Sodium:	76 mg.
Carbohydrate:	5 g.	Calcium:	52 mg.
Fat:	1 g.	Exchanges:	1 vegetable

Nutty Cauliflower ▶ & Carrots

2 cups frozen cauliflowerets
1 cup cooked wild rice,
   page 111
⅓ cup chopped carrot
1 tablespoon slivered almonds
1 tablespoon reduced-calorie
   margarine
¼ teaspoon dried thyme leaves

4 servings

In 2-quart casserole, combine all ingredients. Mix well. Cover. Microwave at High for 8 to 9 minutes, or until carrot is tender-crisp, stirring after half the time.

Per Serving:	
Calories:	88
Protein:	3 g.
Carbohydrate:	14 g.
Fat:	5 g.
Cholesterol:	—
Sodium:	36 mg.
Calcium:	—
Exchanges:	½ starch, 1 vegetable, ½ fat

Corn on the Cob

Spicy Buttery Sauce:
¼ cup reconstituted natural
   butter-flavored mix
1 teaspoon minced green onion
⅛ teaspoon chili powder
   Dash garlic powder
3 to 4 drops hot pepper sauce

Buttery Herb Sauce: (Pictured)
¼ cup reconstituted natural
   butter-flavored mix
1 clove garlic, minced
½ teaspoon snipped fresh
   parsley
⅛ teaspoon dry mustard
⅛ teaspoon Italian seasoning

4 ears fresh corn, husked,
   about 8 oz. each

4 servings

In 1-cup measure, blend all sauce ingredients for either recipe. Set aside.

Place each ear of corn in sheet of plastic wrap. Spread about two teaspoonfuls sauce on each ear. Wrap and twist ends of plastic wrap securely. Microwave at High for 12 to 20 minutes, or until kernels are tender, rearranging and turning ears over after every 4 minutes. Let stand, covered, for 5 minutes. Serve with any remaining sauce.

Per Serving:	
Calories:	89
Protein:	2 g.
Carbohydrate:	21 g.
Fat:	1 g.
Cholesterol:	—
Sodium:	118 mg.
Calcium:	—
Exchanges:	1½ starch

Cucumber & Corn Sauté

2 tablespoons reduced-calorie
   margarine
2 tablespoons sliced green
   onion
½ teaspoon dried basil leaves
1 cup frozen whole kernel corn
1 medium cucumber, peeled,
   seeded and chopped
1 tablespoon chopped pimiento
¼ teaspoon dry mustard
⅛ teaspoon pepper

4 servings

In 1½-quart casserole, combine margarine, onion and basil. Cover. Microwave at High for 1½ to 2½ minutes, or until onion is tender. Stir in remaining ingredients. Re-cover. Microwave at High for 4 to 6 minutes longer, or until cucumber is tender, stirring after every 2 minutes.

Per Serving:			
Calories:	70	Cholesterol:	—
Protein:	2 g.	Sodium:	70 mg.
Carbohydrate:	11 g.	Calcium:	20 mg.
Fat:	3 g.	Exchanges:	½ starch, 1 vegetable

Stuffed Eggplant

1½ cups water
½ cup bulgur or cracked
   wheat
1 pkg. (10 oz.) frozen
   chopped spinach
1 eggplant, about 1½ lbs.
2 tablespoons grated carrot
¼ teaspoon salt*
⅛ teaspoon fennel seed,
   crushed
¼ cup water
2 teaspoons grated Parmesan
   cheese
⅛ teaspoon paprika

6 servings

Place 1½ cups water in 2-cup measure. Microwave at High for 2 to 5 minutes, or until water boils. Place bulgur in small mixing bowl. Add boiling water. Cover and let stand for 30 minutes to soften. Drain and press out excess moisture. Set aside.

Unwrap spinach and place on plate. Microwave at High for 4 to 5 minutes, or until defrosted. Drain and press out excess moisture. Set aside. Cut eggplant in half lengthwise. Scoop out pulp, leaving ¼-inch shell. Place shells in 10-inch square casserole. Set aside. Chop eggplant pulp coarsely. In medium mixing bowl, combine pulp, carrot, salt, fennel and ¼ cup water. Stir. Cover with plastic wrap. Microwave at High for 3 to 5 minutes, or until eggplant is just tender. Drain. Stir in bulgur and spinach. Spoon mixture into eggplant shells. In small bowl, combine Parmesan cheese and paprika. Sprinkle on eggplant. Cover with wax paper. Microwave at 70% (Medium High) for 10 to 15 minutes, or until tender, rotating dish once. Let stand, covered, for 5 minutes.

*To reduce sodium omit salt.

Per Serving:			
Calories:	111	Cholesterol:	—
Protein:	5 g.	Sodium:	287 mg.
Carbohydrate:	23 g.	Calcium:	133 mg.**
Fat:	1 g.	Exchanges:	1 starch, 1½ vegetable

Lettuce-Carrot Sauté ▲

½ cup julienne carrots
   (2 × ⅛-inch strips)
2 tablespoons reduced-calorie
   margarine
1 teaspoon dried coriander
   leaves
4 cups shredded lettuce
1 cup seedless green grapes,
   cut in half
¼ teaspoon salt*

4 servings

In 2-quart casserole, combine
carrots, margarine and coriander.
Cover. Microwave at High for 2
to 3 minutes, or until carrots are
tender-crisp, stirring once after
half the time. Add remaining
ingredients. Stir. Re-cover.
Microwave at High for 2 to 3
minutes longer, or just until
lettuce begins to wilt.

*To reduce sodium omit salt.

Per Serving:	
Calories:	67
Protein:	1 g.
Carbohydrate:	10 g.
Fat:	3 g.
Cholesterol:	—
Sodium:	213 mg.
Calcium:	23 mg.
Exchanges:	2 vegetable, ½ fat

Creamed Leeks

½ lb. leeks, cut in half
   lengthwise, then cut into
   3-inch pieces
¼ cup water
1 tablespoon reconstituted
   natural butter-flavored mix

2 teaspoons cornstarch
¾ cup skim milk
¼ teaspoon dried rosemary
   leaves, crushed
¼ teaspoon low-sodium instant
   chicken bouillon granules

4 servings

In 1-quart casserole, combine leeks and water. Cover. Microwave
at High for 4 to 6 minutes, or until tender-crisp. Drain. Let stand,
covered, while preparing sauce.

In small mixing bowl, blend butter-flavored mix and cornstarch.
Blend in remaining ingredients. Microwave at High for 3 to 4
minutes, or until mixture boils, stirring 2 or 3 times. Reduce power
to 70% (Medium High). Microwave for 1 minute longer. Pour over
leeks. Stir. Re-cover. Microwave at High for 1 minute, or until
heated through.

Per Serving:			
Calories:	57	Cholesterol:	1 mg.
Protein:	3 g.	Sodium:	53 mg.
Carbohydrate:	11 g.	Calcium:	81 mg.**
Fat:	—	Exchanges:	2 vegetable

Slim Twice-baked Potatoes

2 medium baking potatoes
¼ cup dry curd cottage cheese
¼ cup buttermilk
2 teaspoons dry natural
　　butter-flavored mix
1 teaspoon snipped fresh
　　parsley
½ teaspoon freeze-dried chives
¼ teaspoon onion powder
　　Dash pepper
2 teaspoons bacon-flavored
　　soy bits, divided

4 servings

Pierce potatoes with fork.
Arrange on paper towel.
Microwave at High for 6½ to 8
minutes, or until tender, turning
potatoes over and rearranging
after half the time. Wrap in foil.
Let stand for 10 minutes.

Cut each potato in half lengthwise. Scoop out pulp, leaving
¼-inch shell. Place pulp in
medium mixing bowl. Arrange
shells on paper towel-lined
plate. Set aside.

In food processor or blender
bowl, combine cottage cheese
and buttermilk. Process until
smooth. In medium mixing bowl,
combine potato pulp, cottage
cheese mixture, butter-flavored
mix, parsley, chives, onion
powder and pepper. Beat until
smooth and fluffy. Spoon mixture
into potato shells. Microwave at
High for 3 to 4 minutes, or until
heated through, rotating plate
once. Sprinkle with
bacon-flavored bits.

Per Serving:	
Calories:	96
Protein:	4 g.
Carbohydrate:	19 g.
Fat:	1 g.
Cholesterol:	1 mg.
Sodium:	92 mg.
Calcium:	—
Exchanges:	1 starch, 1 vegetable

Mexican Rice-stuffed Peppers

2 medium green peppers, cut
   in half lengthwise, seeded
2 tablespoons water
2 oz. Neufchâtel cheese or
   low-calorie cream cheese
1 tablespoon skim milk
2 cups cooked brown rice,
   page 111
1 tablespoon chopped canned
   green chilies
1 tablespoon snipped fresh
   parsley
⅛ teaspoon pepper
   Paprika

4 servings

Place green pepper halves in
9-inch square baking dish. Add
water. Cover with plastic wrap.
Microwave at High for 6 to 8
minutes, or until tender. Drain.
Set aside.

Place cheese in medium mixing
bowl. Microwave at 50%
(Medium) for 30 seconds to 1
minute, or until cheese softens.
Add milk. Stir until smooth. Add
rice, chilies, parsley and pepper.
Mix well. Spoon mixture into
pepper halves. Sprinkle with
paprika. Cover with wax paper.
Microwave at 50% (Medium) for
4 to 6 minutes, or until heated
through, rotating dish after half
the time.

Per Serving:	
Calories:	157
Protein:	2 g.
Carbohydrate:	25 g.
Fat:	4 g.
Cholesterol:	—
Sodium:	11 mg.
Calcium:	—
Exchanges:	1 starch, 2 vegetable, ½ fat

Italian Potatoes with Fennel ▲

3 tablespoons reduced-calorie
  Italian dressing
2 tablespoons sliced green
  onion
1 tablespoon snipped fresh
  parsley
⅛ teaspoon fennel seed,
  crushed

Dash pepper
2 medium white potatoes,
  sliced ¼ inch thick
1 tablespoon grated Parmesan
  cheese

4 servings

In 2-quart casserole, combine all ingredients, except potatoes and
Parmesan cheese. Stir. Add potatoes. Mix well. Cover. Microwave
at High for 9 to 12 minutes, or until tender, stirring twice. Let stand,
covered, for 4 minutes. Stir. Sprinkle with Parmesan cheese.

Per Serving:			
Calories:	87	Cholesterol:	2 mg.
Protein:	2 g.	Sodium:	116 mg.
Carbohydrate:	17 g.	Calcium:	—
Fat:	1 g.	Exchanges:	1 starch

Tropical Yams

1¼ lbs. fresh yams or sweet
  potatoes
2 tablespoons frozen
  pineapple-orange juice
  concentrate
1 tablespoon reduced-calorie
  margarine

4 servings

Peel yams. Cut into ¼-inch
slices. In 1-quart casserole,
combine yams, pineapple-
orange juice concentrate and
margarine. Stir. Cover. Microwave at High for 10 to 13
minutes, or until tender, stirring
2 or 3 times. Let stand,
covered, for 2 minutes.

Per Serving:	
Calories:	176
Protein:	2 g.
Carbohydrate:	39 g.
Fat:	2 g.
Cholesterol:	—
Sodium:	46 mg.
Calcium:	25 mg.
Exchanges:	2½ starch

Spinach & Sprout Sauté ▲

8 oz. fresh spinach, trimmed
    and coarsely chopped
1½ cups fresh bean sprouts
3 tablespoons chopped
    pecans
1 tablespoon reconstituted
    natural butter-flavored mix
1 teaspoon grated orange
    peel
⅛ teaspoon ground nutmeg

4 servings

In 2-quart casserole, combine
all ingredients. Toss to coat.
Cover. Microwave at High for
5 to 7 minutes, or until spinach
is tender, stirring once. Let
stand, covered, for 3 minutes.

Per Serving:	
Calories:	55
Protein:	2 g.
Carbohydrate:	5 g.
Fat:	4 g.
Cholesterol:	—
Sodium:	50 mg.
Calcium:	—
Exchanges:	1 vegetable, ½ fat

Pineapple Squash

1 medium acorn squash,
    about 1½ lbs.
1 can (8 oz.) unsweetened
    crushed pineapple, drained
1 tablespoon packed brown
    sugar
1 tablespoon chopped pecans
1 tablespoon reconstituted
    natural butter-flavored mix
⅛ teaspoon dry mustard
⅛ teaspoon ground nutmeg
    Dash ground allspice

4 servings

Cut squash in half crosswise.
Scoop out seeds. Cut each
piece in half lengthwise. Place
in 9-inch square baking dish.
Set aside. In small mixing bowl,
combine remaining ingredients.
Spoon mixture into squash
quarters. Cover with plastic
wrap. Microwave at High for 8
to 12 minutes, or until squash is
tender, rotating dish once. Let
stand, covered, for 3 minutes.

Per Serving:	
Calories:	118
Protein:	2 g.
Carbohydrate:	19 g.
Fat:	1 g.
Cholesterol:	—
Sodium:	33 mg.
Calcium:	—
Exchanges:	1 starch, 1 vegetable

Quick Couscous
& Zucchini

1 medium zucchini, cut into
    2 × ¼-inch strips
2 tablespoons sliced green
    onion
1 tablespoon snipped fresh
    parsley
2 tablespoons reduced-sodium
    soy sauce
2 tablespoons white wine
    Dash garlic powder
    Dash ground ginger
½ cup uncooked couscous
½ cup water
1 tablespoon reduced-calorie
    margarine

4 servings

In 1½-quart casserole, combine
zucchini, onion, parsley, soy
sauce, wine, garlic powder and
ginger. Stir. Cover. Microwave at
High for 2 to 3 minutes, or until
color brightens on zucchini. Stir
in remaining ingredients.
Re-cover. Microwave at High for
2½ to 4 minutes longer, or until
mixture boils. Let stand, covered,
for 3 minutes. Toss lightly.

Per Serving:	
Calories:	100
Protein:	3 g.
Carbohydrate:	17 g.
Fat:	4 g.
Cholesterol:	—
Sodium:	284 mg.
Calcium:	—
Exchanges:	1 starch, ½ vegetable, ½ fat

Summer Vegetable Combo

1 pkg. (10 oz.) frozen cut green
    beans
8 oz. crookneck squash, sliced
    ¼ inch thick
2 tablespoons water
2 tablespoons reduced-calorie
    margarine
½ teaspoon dried parsley flakes
¼ teaspoon onion powder
⅛ teaspoon dried oregano
    leaves
⅛ teaspoon garlic powder
    Dash pepper

6 servings

In 1½-quart casserole, combine
beans, squash and water. Cover.
Microwave at High for 7 to 11
minutes, or until vegetables are
tender-crisp, stirring twice. Set
vegetables aside.

In 1-cup measure, combine
remaining ingredients. Mix well.
Microwave at 70% (Medium
High) for 20 to 30 seconds, or
just until margarine melts. Drain
vegetables. Pour margarine
mixture over vegetables. Stir
to coat.

Per Serving:
Calories:	57
Protein:	2 g.
Carbohydrate:	7 g.
Fat:	5 g.
Cholesterol:	—
Sodium:	39 mg.
Calcium:	43 mg.
Exchanges:	1 vegetable, 1 fat

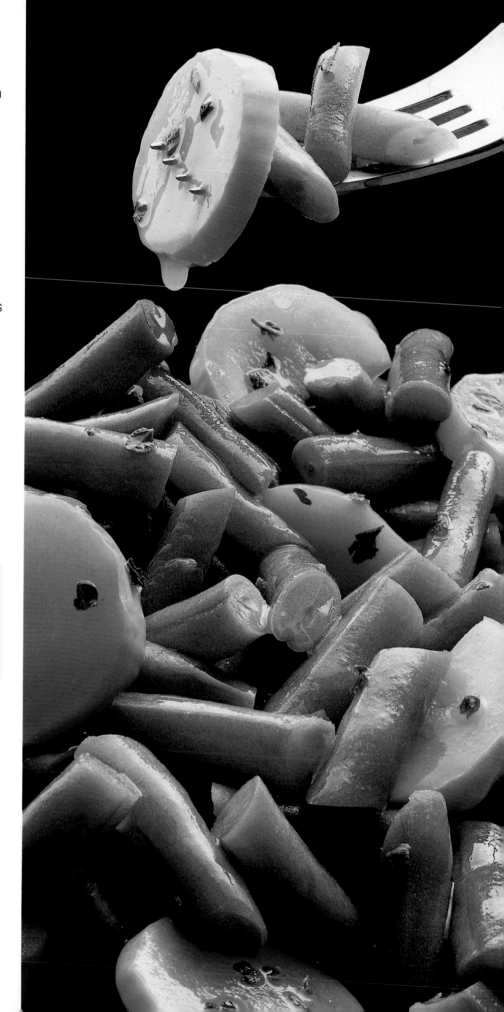

◀ Steamed Chinese Vegetables

2 tablespoons reduced-sodium soy sauce
1 teaspoon sugar
½ teaspoon sesame seed
1 clove garlic, minced
2 cups chopped Chinese cabbage
2 stalks bok choy, sliced ¼ inch thick, leafy part sliced ½ inch thick
1 cup fresh bean sprouts
8 cherry tomatoes, cut in half lengthwise

4 servings

In 2-quart casserole, blend soy sauce, sugar, sesame and garlic. Stir in Chinese cabbage and bok choy. Cover. Microwave at High for 4 to 5 minutes, or until tender-crisp, stirring once. Stir in bean sprouts and tomatoes. Re-cover. Microwave at High for 1 to 2 minutes longer, or until bean sprouts are tender-crisp.

Per Serving:
Calories:	26
Protein:	1 g.
Carbohydrate:	6 g.
Fat:	2 g.
Cholesterol:	—
Sodium:	270 mg.
Calcium:	—
Exchanges:	1 vegetable

Stuffed Tomatoes ▲

4 medium fresh tomatoes
3 small white potatoes, thinly sliced, about 12 oz.
2 tablespoons chopped onion
2 tablespoons water
½ cup part-skim ricotta cheese
3 tablespoons skim milk
1 tablespoon snipped fresh parsley
¼ teaspoon dried basil leaves
⅛ teaspoon salt*
⅛ teaspoon pepper
2 tablespoons finely grated carrot

4 servings

Remove slice from stem end of tomatoes. Scoop out pulp. Place tomato shells upside down in 9-inch square baking dish. Set aside.

In 1-quart casserole, combine potatoes, onion and water. Cover. Microwave at High for 5 to 10 minutes, or until tender, stirring once. Place potato mixture in medium mixing bowl. Add remaining ingredients, except carrot. Beat until smooth. Stir in carrot. Spoon mixture into tomato shells. Microwave at High for 4 to 8 minutes, or until tomatoes are heated through, rearranging once.

*To reduce sodium omit salt.

Per Serving:
Calories:	164	Cholesterol:	10 mg.
Protein:	7 g.	Sodium:	120 mg.
Carbohydrate:	29 g.	Calcium:	115 mg.**
Fat:	3 g.	Exchanges:	1½ starch, 1 vegetable, ½ fat

Pasta & Grains

◄ Hot Pasta Salad

1 medium green pepper, cut
  into ¼-inch strips
½ medium red onion, cut in half
  lengthwise and thinly sliced
2 tablespoons reconstituted
  natural butter-flavored mix
2 teaspoons poppy seed
⅛ teaspoon salt*
¾ cup cooked spaghetti
1 medium tomato, cut into thin
  wedges

4 servings

In 1-quart casserole, combine
all ingredients, except spaghetti
and tomato. Cover. Microwave
at High for 3 to 5 minutes, or
just until pepper and onion
are tender, stirring once. Add
remaining ingredients. Toss
lightly. Re-cover. Microwave at
High for 2 to 3 minutes longer,
or until hot. Let stand, covered,
for 1 minute.

*To reduce sodium omit salt.

Per Serving:	
Calories:	65
Protein:	2 g.
Carbohydrate:	14 g.
Fat:	—
Cholesterol:	—
Sodium:	115 mg.
Calcium:	—
Exchanges:	½ starch, 1 vegetable

Garlic Rice & Pasta

2 tablespoons reduced-calorie
  margarine
1 cup uncooked brown rice
½ cup uncooked broken
  spaghetti
3 cups hot water
2 tablespoons sliced green
  onion
1 clove garlic, minced
½ teaspoon salt*
⅛ teaspoon pepper
2 tablespoons snipped fresh
  parsley

8 servings

In 3-quart casserole, combine
margarine, rice and spaghetti.
Microwave at High for 4 to 7
minutes, or until spaghetti is
golden brown, stirring after first
2 minutes, then after every
minute. Stir in remaining ingredients, except parsley. Cover.
Microwave at High for 5
minutes. Reduce power to 50%
(Medium). Microwave for 35 to
40 minutes longer, or until liquid
is absorbed and rice is tender.
Add parsley. Let stand, covered,
for 5 minutes. Toss lightly.

*To reduce sodium omit salt.

Per Serving:	
Calories:	92
Protein:	2 g.
Carbohydrate:	16 g.
Fat:	4 g.
Cholesterol:	—
Sodium:	154 mg.
Calcium:	—
Exchanges:	1 starch, ½ fat

Rice Medley

½ cup uncooked brown rice
¼ cup uncooked wild rice,
  rinsed and drained
¼ cup chopped green or red
  pepper
2 tablespoons snipped fresh
  parsley
1 tablespoon finely chopped
  celery
2¼ cups hot water
2 tablespoons white wine
1 teaspoon low-sodium instant
  beef bouillon granules
¼ teaspoon salt*
¼ teaspoon bouquet garni
  seasoning
1 bay leaf

6 servings

In 2-quart casserole, combine
all ingredients. Mix well. Cover.
Microwave at High for 5
minutes. Reduce power to 50%
(Medium). Microwave for 45 to
55 minutes longer, or until liquid
is absorbed and rice is tender.
Let stand, covered, for 5
minutes. Remove bay leaf.
Toss lightly.

*To reduce sodium omit salt.

Per Serving:	
Calories:	87
Protein:	2 g.
Carbohydrate:	18 g.
Fat:	—
Cholesterol:	—
Sodium:	133 mg.
Calcium:	—
Exchanges:	1 starch, ½ vegetable

Barley-Rice Pilaf ▲

⅓ cup quick-cooking barley
¼ cup uncooked brown rice
1⅔ cups hot water
1 cup sliced fresh mushrooms
¼ cup (¼-inch cubes) carrot
2 tablespoons snipped fresh
   parsley
1 clove garlic, minced
1 teaspoon lemon juice
½ teaspoon dried thyme
   leaves

6 servings

In 2-quart casserole, combine
all ingredients. Mix well. Cover.
Microwave at High for 5 minutes.
Reduce power to 50% (Medium).
Microwave for 35 to 45 minutes
longer, or until liquid is
absorbed and rice is tender. Let
stand, covered, for 5 minutes.

Per Serving:	
Calories:	62
Protein:	2 g.
Carbohydrate:	14 g.
Fat:	—
Cholesterol:	—
Sodium:	7 mg.
Calcium:	—
Exchanges:	½ starch, 1 vegetable

Barley & Black-eyed Peas

1 tablespoon reduced-calorie
   margarine
½ cup sliced carrot, ¼ inch
   thick
¼ cup sliced green onions
1 cup ready-to-serve
   low-sodium chicken broth
⅓ cup quick-cooking barley
1 tablespoon snipped fresh
   parsley
¼ teaspoon salt*
⅛ teaspoon pepper
1 can (16 oz.) black-eyed peas,
   rinsed and drained

4 servings

In 2-quart casserole, combine margarine, carrot and onions. Cover.
Microwave at High for 3 to 6 minutes, or until tender, stirring after
half the time. Add remaining ingredients, except black-eyed peas.
Mix well. Re-cover. Microwave at High for 13 to 15 minutes longer,
or until liquid is absorbed and the barley is tender. Stir in black-
eyed peas. Re-cover. Microwave at High for 2 minutes, or until
heated through.

*To reduce sodium omit salt.

Per Serving:			
Calories:	177	Cholesterol:	—
Protein:	7 g.	Sodium:	456 mg.
Carbohydrate:	32 g.	Calcium:	—
Fat:	6 g.	Exchanges:	2 starch, ½ vegetable, ½ fat

Bulgur Pilaf

3 cups water
1 cup bulgur or cracked wheat
½ cup chopped carrot
¼ cup chopped onion
2 tablespoons snipped fresh
  parsley
1 clove garlic, minced
1 teaspoon dried chervil leaves
⅛ teaspoon pepper
2 tablespoons reduced-calorie
  margarine
1 cup frozen peas
1 tablespoon grated Parmesan
  cheese
¼ teaspoon salt*

8 servings

Place water in 4-cup measure. Microwave at High for 4 to 9 minutes, or until water boils. Place bulgur in medium mixing bowl. Add boiling water. Cover and let stand for 30 minutes to soften. Drain and press out excess moisture. Set aside.

In 2-quart casserole, combine carrot, onion, parsley, garlic, chervil, pepper and margarine. Cover. Microwave at High for 4 to 5 minutes, or until vegetables are tender, stirring after half the time. Add bulgur, peas, Parmesan cheese and salt. Mix well. Re-cover. Microwave at High for 2 to 4½ minutes longer, or until heated through.

*To reduce sodium omit salt.

Per Serving:
Calories: 141
Protein: 4 g.
Carbohydrate: 24 g.
Fat: 5 g.
Cholesterol: —
Sodium: 121 mg.
Calcium: 18 mg.
Exchanges: 1½ starch, 1 fat

Tomato-Cheese Grits ▲

2 tablespoons reduced-calorie
  margarine
2 tablespoons sliced green
  onion
1 clove garlic, minced
¼ teaspoon salt*
⅛ teaspoon pepper

1¾ cups hot water
½ cup quick-cooking grits
1 medium tomato, seeded
  and chopped
¼ cup shredded Cheddar
  cheese

4 servings

In 2-quart casserole, combine margarine, onion and garlic. Microwave at High for 1½ to 2 minutes, or until tender. Add salt, pepper and water. Microwave at High for 3 to 6 minutes, or until water boils. Stir in grits and tomato. Microwave at High for 4 to 5 minutes, or until liquid is absorbed and grits are tender, stirring after half the time. Stir in Cheddar cheese.

*To reduce sodium omit salt.

Per Serving:
Calories: 96.5   Cholesterol: 7 mg.
Protein: 3 g.   Sodium: 360 mg.
Carbohydrate: 8 g.   Calcium: 55 mg.
Fat: 9 g.   Exchanges: ½ starch, 1½ fat

Polenta

2 cups hot water
½ cup ready-to-serve
    low-sodium chicken broth
1 tablespoon snipped fresh
    parsley
¼ teaspoon salt*
⅛ teaspoon dried marjoram
    leaves
    Dash pepper
1 cup yellow cornmeal
3 tablespoons grated
    Parmesan cheese
2 tablespoons reduced-calorie
    margarine
    Vegetable cooking spray
1 cup Basic Tomato Sauce,
    page 98

8 servings

In 2-quart measure, combine water, broth, parsley, salt, marjoram and pepper. Microwave at High for 5 to 8 minutes, or until mixture boils. Slowly whisk in cornmeal, cheese and margarine, stirring just until margarine melts. Reduce power to 50% (Medium). Microwave for 5 to 10 minutes longer, or until mixture is very thick, stirring once or twice.

Spray 8 × 4-inch loaf dish with vegetable cooking spray. Spread polenta evenly into prepared dish. Chill for 30 minutes, or until warm but set. Invert dish. Cut polenta into 16 slices. Arrange slices in 9-inch square baking dish, overlapping as necessary. Pour tomato sauce over polenta. Cover with wax paper. Microwave at High for 4 to 7 minutes, or until heated through, rotating dish once.

*To reduce sodium omit salt.

Per Serving:
Calories: 108
Protein: 3 g.
Carbohydrate: 16 g.
Fat: 3 g.
Cholesterol: 2 mg.
Sodium: 270 mg.
Calcium: 55 mg.
Exchanges: 1 starch, ½ fat

Sunny Couscous Cereal ▶

¾ cup water
¼ cup fresh orange juice
½ cup uncooked couscous
1 teaspoon grated orange peel
2 tablespoons finely chopped
    blanched almonds
1 tablespoon honey
1 tablespoon frozen apple juice
    concentrate
    Dash ground cinnamon

4 servings

In 1-quart casserole, combine all
ingredients. Cover. Microwave
at High for 5 to 6 minutes, or
until liquid is absorbed and
couscous is tender. Let stand,
covered, for 1 minute.

Per Serving:	
Calories:	122
Protein:	3 g.
Carbohydrate:	23 g.
Fat:	2 g.
Cholesterol:	—
Sodium:	1 mg.
Calcium:	—
Exchanges:	1 starch, ½ fruit, ½ fat

Spiced Creamy Cereal

2 cups skim milk
⅓ cup regular cream of wheat
    cereal
2 tablespoons chopped dried
    apricots
⅛ teaspoon salt*
    Dash ground nutmeg
    Dash ground allspice

2 servings

In 2-quart casserole, combine
all ingredients. Microwave at
High for 6 to 8 minutes, or until
cereal thickens, stirring after
every 2 minutes.

*To reduce sodium omit salt.

Per Serving:	
Calories:	78
Protein:	5 g.
Carbohydrate:	13 g.
Fat:	—
Cholesterol:	5 mg.
Sodium:	171 mg.
Calcium:	196 mg.**
Exchanges:	½ starch, ½ skim milk

Oatmeal with Prunes & Raisins

2½ cups hot water
1⅓ cups old-fashioned rolled
    oats
¼ cup instant nonfat
    dry milk powder
¼ cup chopped pitted prunes
2 tablespoons raisins
2 teaspoons dry natural
    butter-flavored mix
¼ teaspoon salt*
¼ teaspoon ground cinnamon

4 servings

In 2-quart casserole, combine all ingredients. Mix well. Microwave
at High for 8 to 10 minutes, or until desired consistency, stirring
after half the time.

*To reduce sodium omit salt.

Per Serving:			
Calories:	172	Cholesterol:	1 mg.
Protein:	7 g.	Sodium:	582 mg.
Carbohydrate:	32 g.	Calcium:	80 mg.**
Fat:	—	Exchanges:	1½ starch, ½ fruit

◄ Raspberry Cheese Cooler

3 oz. Neufchâtel cheese or
  low-calorie cream cheese
1 envelope (1.4 oz.) whipped
  dessert topping mix
Skim milk
1½ cups water
1 pkg. (6 oz.) sugar-free
  raspberry gelatin
1 can (12 oz.) sugar-free
  lemon lime soda
2 cups frozen unsweetened
  raspberries

10 servings

Place cheese in small bowl. Microwave at 50% (Medium) for 30 seconds to 1 minute, or until cheese softens. Stir until smooth. Set aside. In small mixing bowl, prepare dessert topping as directed on package, using skim milk. Beat in softened cheese. Set aside.

Place water in 2-cup measure. Microwave at High for 4 to 6 minutes, or until water boils. Place gelatin in large mixing bowl. Add boiling water. Stir until gelatin dissolves. Stir in soda. Blend ½ cup gelatin mixture into topping mixture. Set aside. Add raspberries to remaining gelatin mixture. Chill until slightly thickened. Pour into 9-inch round baking dish. Spread topping evenly over gelatin. Chill for about 3 hours, or until set. Cut into wedges.

Per Serving:	
Calories:	70
Protein:	3 g.
Carbohydrate:	7 g.
Fat:	2 g.
Cholesterol:	11 mg.
Sodium:	25 mg.
Calcium:	54 mg.
Exchanges:	½ med.-fat meat, ½ fruit

Cold Mandarin-Pineapple Soufflé

1 can (16 oz.) mandarin
  oranges, drained (reserve
  6 segments)
½ cup canned unsweetened
  crushed pineapple
½ teaspoon vanilla

1 envelope unflavored gelatine
½ cup water
2 egg whites, room
  temperature
2 tablespoons sugar

6 servings

In food processor or blender bowl, process oranges, pineapple and vanilla until pureed. Place ½ cup puree in small mixing bowl. Sprinkle gelatine over puree in bowl. Let stand for 2 minutes to soften. Reserve remaining puree.

Place water in 1-cup measure. Microwave at High for 45 seconds to 1¼ minutes, or until water boils. Add to gelatine mixture. Stir until gelatine dissolves. Stir in reserved puree. Chill until slightly thickened. To "quick-set," place in freezer for 15 to 20 minutes, stirring 2 or 3 times.

In medium mixing bowl, beat egg whites at high speed of electric mixture until foamy. Beat in sugar, 1 tablespoon at a time, until stiff peaks form. Fold fruit mixture into egg whites. Spoon into six individual dishes. Garnish with reserved orange segments. Chill for at least 2 hours, or until set. Refrigerate for no longer than 2 days.

Per Serving:			
Calories:	65	Cholesterol:	—
Protein:	2 g.	Sodium:	20 mg.
Carbohydrate:	15 g.	Calcium:	—
Fat:	—	Exchanges:	1 fruit

Cheater's Cheesecake

Crust:
3 tablespoons regular
   margarine
1 cup graham cracker crumbs
2 tablespoons sugar

Filling:
1 carton (15 oz.) part-skim
   ricotta cheese

1 cup low-fat plain yogurt
3 egg whites
⅓ cup sugar
1 teaspoon vanilla
½ teaspoon almond extract

Topping:
10 fresh strawberries

10 servings

Place margarine in 9-inch round baking dish. Microwave at High for 45 seconds to 1 minute, or until margarine melts. Stir in graham cracker crumbs and sugar. Press firmly against bottom of dish. Microwave at High for 1½ to 2 minutes, or until set, rotating dish after 1 minute. Set aside.

In medium mixing bowl, combine all filling ingredients. Beat at high speed of electric mixer until smooth. Microwave at High for 4 to 7 minutes, or until very hot, stirring with whisk after every 2 minutes. Pour into prepared crust. Microwave at 50% (Medium) for 7 to 15 minutes, or until center is almost set, rotating dish ¼ turn after every 3 minutes. (Filling will become firm as it chills.) Cool slightly. Chill for at least 6 hours. Garnish with strawberry fans.

Cut each strawberry lengthwise into thin slices, almost to stem.

Fan each strawberry slightly. Place on each serving.

Per Serving:			
Calories:	186	Cholesterol:	17 mg.
Protein:	8 g.	Sodium:	167 mg.
Carbohydrate:	20 g.	Calcium:	183 mg.**
Fat:	8 g.	Exchanges:	½ starch, ½ fruit, ½ skim milk, 1½ fat

1 bag (16 oz.) frozen whole
    strawberries
2 cups cold water, divided
1 pkg. (3 oz.) sugar-free
    strawberry gelatin
1 cup buttermilk
14 (3 oz. each) paper cups
14 flat wooden sticks

14 servings

Place strawberries in large
bowl. Microwave at High for
2 minutes. Let stand for 5 to
10 minutes. Chop into small
pieces. Set aside.

Place 1 cup water in 4-cup
measure. Microwave at High for
2½ to 3½ minutes, or until water
boils. Place gelatin in large
mixing bowl. Add boiling water.
Stir until gelatin dissolves. Stir in
1 cup cold water and the buttermilk. Add strawberries. Mix well.
Freeze for about 1 hour, or until
slightly thickened, stirring twice.
Pour into paper cups to within
¼ inch from top. Place cups in
13 × 9-inch pan. Insert wooden
sticks in center of each cup.
Freeze until firm. Peel off paper
cup before serving.

Per Serving:	
Calories:	24
Protein:	3 g.
Carbohydrate:	5 g.
Fat:	—
Cholesterol:	—
Sodium:	19 mg.
Calcium:	20 mg.
Exchanges:	½ fruit

Minted Fruit Compote

2 nectarines, pitted and sliced
2 plums, pitted and quartered
1 cup water
¾ cup halved red or green
    seedless grapes
2 tablespoons quick-cooking
    tapioca

2 tablespoons frozen apple
    juice concentrate
1 teaspoon honey
½ teaspoon dried mint leaves

8 servings, ½ cup each

In 2-quart casserole, combine all ingredients. Microwave at High
for 14 to 21 minutes, or until tapioca is tender and translucent,
stirring twice. Chill for at least 3 hours. Serve cool.

Per Serving:			
Calories:	51	Cholesterol:	—
Protein:	1 g.	Sodium:	1 mg.
Carbohydrate:	12 g.	Calcium:	5 mg.
Fat:	—	Exchanges:	1 fruit

Curried Stewed Fruit ▲

2 small oranges
1 cup pitted chopped prunes
1 cup dried sliced apples
½ cup water
½ cup apple juice
⅓ cup raisins
1 tablespoon honey
⅛ teaspoon curry powder

6 servings

Remove peel and white membrane from oranges. Cut sections from inside membrane and place in small mixing bowl. Squeeze any remaining juice from membrane over oranges. Set aside. In 1½-quart casserole, combine remaining ingredients. Mix well. Cover. Microwave at High for 4 to 7 minutes, or until fruit is plump and tender, stirring after every 2 minutes. Stir in orange sections and juice. Let stand, covered, for 5 minutes before serving.

Per Serving:
Calories:	128
Protein:	1 g.
Carbohydrate:	33 g.
Fat:	—
Cholesterol:	—
Sodium:	—
Calcium:	35 mg.
Exchanges:	2 fruit

Ginger Fruit Boats

1 fresh pineapple, about 3 lbs.
1 can (16 oz.) pitted dark sweet cherries, drained
1 can (16 oz.) apricot halves, in light syrup, drained
½ cup low-sugar orange marmalade
1 tablespoon honey
1 teaspoon chopped crystallized ginger

4 servings

Cut pineapple into quarters, lengthwise through crown. Remove fruit with serrated fruit knife, leaving ½-inch shell. Reserve shells. Cut fruit into small chunks. Place in medium mixing bowl. Stir in cherries and apricots. Set aside.

In 2-cup measure, combine marmalade, honey and ginger. Microwave at High for 1½ to 3 minutes, or until mixture boils, stirring after half the time. Pour over fruit. Cover. Chill for 3 to 4 hours, stirring once. Mound one-fourth of fruit mixture on each pineapple shell.

Per Serving:
Calories:	240	Cholesterol:	—
Protein:	3 g.	Sodium:	—
Carbohydrate:	64 g.	Calcium:	55 mg.
Fat:	—	Exchanges:	4 fruit

◄ Easy Peach Raisin Crisp

1 bag (16 oz.) frozen sliced
   peaches
¼ cup raisins
1 tablespoon lemon juice
¾ teaspoon apple pie spice
½ cup rolled oats
½ cup whole wheat flour
3 tablespoons packed brown
   sugar
2 tablespoons chopped pecans
¼ cup regular margarine
9 tablespoons Honey Yogurt,
   right, divided

9 servings

Place peaches in 9-inch square
baking dish. Microwave at 50%
(Medium) for 4 to 8 minutes, or
until defrosted, stirring once. Let
stand for 5 to 10 minutes. Drain.
Stir in raisins, lemon juice and
apple pie spice. Spread evenly
over bottom of dish. Set aside.

In small mixing bowl, combine
rolled oats, flour, brown sugar
and pecans. Cut in margarine
to form coarse crumbs. Spread
over fruit mixture. Microwave at
High for 6 to 10 minutes, or until
peaches are tender and mixture
bubbles around edges. Serve
warm with Honey Yogurt on
each serving.

Per Serving:
Calories: 167
Protein: 3 g.
Carbohydrate: 25 g.
Fat: 7 g.
Cholesterol: 1 mg.
Sodium: 136 mg.
Calcium: 45 mg.
Exchanges: ½ starch, 1 fruit, 1½ fat

Chocolate Yogurt ▲

1⅔ cups instant nonfat dry milk
   powder
3¾ cups water
2 teaspoons vanilla
⅓ cup low-fat plain yogurt
⅓ cup chocolate syrup

8 servings, ½ cup each

In 2-quart casserole, blend dry
milk and water with whisk. Stir in
vanilla. Microwave at High for 8
to 14 minutes, or until temperature registers 190°F, stirring after
half the time. Cool to 115°F.
Blend in plain yogurt and
chocolate syrup. Cover with
plastic wrap. Insert microwave
thermometer through center of
plastic wrap. Allow mixture to
stand in microwave oven
undisturbed for 2 to 4 hours.
Check temperature after every
30 minutes. If temperature falls
below 110°F, microwave at 30%
(Medium Low) for 30 seconds
to 2 minutes, or until temperature registers 115°F. Mixture will
appear set. Chill for several
hours. Stir before serving.

Per Serving:
Calories: 91
Protein: 6 g.
Carbohydrate: 17 g.
Fat: 1 g.
Cholesterol: 5 mg.
Sodium: 88 mg.
Calcium: 193 mg.**
Exchanges: ½ skim milk, ½ fruit

Honey Yogurt

1⅔ cups instant nonfat dry milk
   powder
3¾ cups water
¼ cup honey
2 teaspoons vanilla
⅓ cup low-fat plain yogurt

8 servings, ½ cup each

In 2-quart casserole, blend dry
milk and water with whisk. Stir in
honey and vanilla. Microwave at
High for 8 to 14 minutes, or until
temperature registers 190°F,
stirring after half the time. Cool
to 115°F. Blend in plain yogurt.
Cover with plastic wrap. Insert
microwave thermometer through
center of plastic wrap. Allow
mixture to stand in microwave
oven undisturbed for 2 to 4
hours. Check temperature after
every 30 minutes. If temperature
falls below 110°F, microwave at
30% (Medium Low) for 30
seconds to 2 minutes, or until
temperature registers 115°F.
Mixture will appear set. Chill for
several hours. Stir yogurt
before serving.

Per Serving:
Calories: 89
Protein: 5 g.
Carbohydrate: 16 g.
Fat: 1 g.
Cholesterol: 5 mg.
Sodium: 81 mg.
Calcium: 191 mg.**
Exchanges: ½ skim milk, ½ fruit

Naturally Good Treats ▲

¾ cup natural no-salt peanut
    butter
¼ cup honey
 3 tablespoons reduced-calorie
    margarine
½ cup instant nonfat dry milk
    powder
½ cup unsalted sunflower nuts
⅓ cup sesame seed
⅓ cup cornflake crumbs
¼ cup finely chopped dried
    apricots
⅔ cup flaked coconut

30 treats

In 1½-quart casserole, combine
peanut butter, honey and
margarine. Microwave at High
for 1 to 2 minutes, or until hot
and mixture can be stirred
smooth. Stir in remaining ingredients, except coconut. Shape
into 30 balls, about 1¼ inches.
Roll each treat in coconut. Chill
for at least 3 hours, or until firm.

Per Serving:	
Calories:	86
Protein:	3 g.
Carbohydrate:	7 g.
Fat:	7 g.
Cholesterol:	—
Sodium:	28 mg.
Calcium:	20 mg.
Exchanges:	½ starch, 1 fat

Maple Custard

 1 egg
 2 egg whites
½ teaspoon vanilla
2¼ cups skim milk
 3 tablespoons pure maple
    syrup
   Ground cardamom
1½ cups fresh blueberries

6 servings

In 1-cup measure, blend egg,
egg whites and vanilla. Set
aside. In 4-cup measure, blend
milk and maple syrup. Microwave at High for 3 to 5 minutes,
or until very hot but not boiling.
Whisk egg mixture into hot milk
in slow steady stream. Pour
mixture into six custard cups.

Arrange cups in circular pattern
in oven. Microwave at 50%
(Medium) for 13 to 22 minutes,
or until soft-set, rearranging 3
times. As custard appears set,
remove from oven. Sprinkle with
cardamom. Serve warm or cool
with blueberries.

Per Serving:	
Calories:	109
Protein:	6 g.
Carbohydrate:	19 g.
Fat:	1 g.
Cholesterol:	48 mg.
Sodium:	89 mg.
Calcium:	142 mg.**
Exchanges:	1 skim milk, ½ fruit

Scandinavian Brown Rice Pudding

 2 cups hot water
⅔ cup uncooked brown rice
 2 tablespoons currants
 2 tablespoons chopped dried
    apricots
 1 tablespoon reduced-calorie
    margarine
 2 teaspoons honey
½ teaspoon peeled, finely
    chopped gingerroot
¼ teaspoon ground cinnamon
⅛ teaspoon ground nutmeg
½ cup skim milk

6 servings, ⅓ cup each

In 2-quart casserole, combine
all ingredients, except milk. Mix
well. Cover. Microwave at High
for 5 minutes. Reduce power to
50% (Medium). Microwave for
40 to 50 minutes longer, or until
liquid is absorbed and rice is
tender. Stir in milk. Serve warm.

Per Serving:	
Calories:	102
Protein:	2 g.
Carbohydrate:	20 g.
Fat:	3 g.
Cholesterol:	—
Sodium:	36 mg.
Calcium:	31 mg.
Exchanges:	½ starch, 1 fruit, ½ fat

Almond-Spice Couscous

¾ cup apple juice
⅔ cup uncooked couscous
¼ teaspoon grated orange peel
⅛ teaspoon ground cardamom
  Dash ground cinnamon
¼ cup sliced almonds
¼ cup low-fat plain yogurt

6 servings, ⅓ cup each

In 1-quart casserole, combine all ingredients, except almonds and yogurt. Mix well. Cover. Microwave at High for 2 minutes, or until liquid is absorbed and couscous is tender. Stir in almonds and yogurt. Serve warm or cool in individual dishes.

Per Serving:	
Calories:	112
Protein:	4 g.
Carbohydrate:	18 g.
Fat:	3 g.
Cholesterol:	1 mg.
Sodium:	1 mg.
Calcium:	36 mg.
Exchanges:	1 starch, ½ fat

Apple Cheese Squares ▼

¾ cup unbleached all-purpose flour
¾ cup whole wheat flour
⅓ cup packed brown sugar
½ teaspoon baking soda
½ teaspoon baking powder
½ teaspoon ground cinnamon
¼ teaspoon ground cardamom
¼ teaspoon ground nutmeg
1⅓ cups unsweetened applesauce
5 tablespoons reduced-calorie margarine, cut-up
1 egg
1 tablespoon frozen orange juice concentrate

Topping:
⅔ cup part-skim ricotta cheese
⅓ cup unsweetened applesauce
2 teaspoons frozen orange juice concentrate

20 servings

In large mixing bowl, combine unbleached flour, whole wheat flour, brown sugar, baking soda, baking powder, cinnamon, cardamom and nutmeg. Mix well. Add applesauce, margarine, egg and orange juice concentrate. Beat at low speed of electric mixer until blended, scraping bowl constantly. Beat at medium speed for 1 minute, scraping bowl frequently. Spread batter into 9-inch square baking dish. Shield corners of dish with triangles of foil.

Place dish on saucer in oven. Microwave at 50% (Medium) for 6 minutes, rotating dish after half the time. Remove foil. Increase power to High. Microwave for 4½ to 6 minutes longer, or until center springs back when touched lightly and no uncooked batter remains on the bottom. Let stand on counter for 10 minutes. Cool completely.

In small mixing bowl, blend all topping ingredients until smooth. Spread evenly over cooled cake. Cut into squares.

Per Serving:			
Calories:	86	Cholesterol:	16 mg.
Protein:	2 g.	Sodium:	72 mg.
Carbohydrate:	13 g.	Calcium:	32 mg.
Fat:	5 g.	Exchanges:	½ starch, ½ fruit, ½ fat

◄ Apple Coffee Cake

Vegetable cooking spray
2 tablespoons graham cracker crumbs
¼ cup reduced-calorie margarine
3 tablespoons packed brown sugar
½ cup low-fat plain yogurt
1 egg white
½ teaspoon vanilla
⅔ cup unbleached all-purpose flour
⅓ cup whole wheat flour
1 teaspoon ground cinnamon
½ teaspoon baking soda
½ teaspoon baking powder
¼ teaspoon ground nutmeg
⅛ teaspoon salt*
⅛ teaspoon ground allspice
⅛ teaspoon ground cardamom
1 medium baking apple, peeled, cored, one-half shredded and one-half cut into thin slices

Topping:
2 tablespoons low-fat plain yogurt
2 teaspoons honey

8 servings

Spray 9-inch ring dish with vegetable cooking spray. Sprinkle with graham cracker crumbs. Tilt dish to coat. Set aside.

In medium mixing bowl, cream margarine and brown sugar until fluffy. Add yogurt, egg white and vanilla. Beat at low speed of electric mixer until blended. Add remaining cake ingredients, except apple. Beat at medium speed for 1 minute, scraping bowl occasionally. Stir in shredded apple. Arrange apple slices in bottom of prepared dish.

Pour batter evenly into dish. Microwave at 70% (Medium High) for 8 to 12 minutes, or until center springs back when touched lightly and no uncooked batter remains on the bottom, rotating dish twice. Let stand on counter for 5 minutes. Loosen edges. Invert onto serving plate.

In small bowl, blend topping ingredients until smooth. Drizzle over warm cake.

*To reduce sodium omit salt.

Per Serving:			
Calories:	115	Cholesterol:	1 mg.
Protein:	2 g.	Sodium:	180 mg.
Carbohydrate:	18 g.	Calcium:	41 mg.
Fat:	8 g.	Exchanges:	½ starch, ½ fruit, 1 fat

Carob Bran Raisin Bars

Vegetable cooking spray
⅔ cup natural no-salt peanut butter
2 tablespoons reduced-calorie margarine
2 tablespoons honey
2 tablespoons light corn syrup
2 tablespoons carob powder
2 cups bran flake cereal, coarsely crushed
⅓ cup chopped raisins
2 tablespoons wheat germ

25 bars

Spray 9-inch square baking dish with vegetable cooking spray. Set aside. In 1½-quart casserole, combine peanut butter, margarine, honey and corn syrup. Microwave at High for 1 to 2 minutes, or until hot and bubbly. Stir until smooth. Stir in carob powder until blended. Mix in cereal, raisins and wheat germ until coated. Press cereal mixture into bottom of prepared dish. Chill for 3 hours. Cut into bars.

Per Serving:	
Calories:	73
Protein:	2 g.
Carbohydrate:	8 g.
Fat:	5 g.
Cholesterol:	—
Sodium:	36 mg.
Calcium:	6 mg.
Exchanges:	½ starch, 1 fat

Carob Chip Bars

¾ cup unbleached all-purpose
    flour
½ cup packed brown sugar
1 teaspoon baking soda
1 teaspoon ground cinnamon
½ teaspoon ground nutmeg
¾ cup shredded carrot
¾ cup shredded zucchini
2 eggs
¼ cup reduced-calorie
    margarine, cut-up
3 tablespoons vegetable oil
½ cup chopped walnuts
¼ cup carob chips

Icing:

2 oz. Neufchâtel cheese or
    low-calorie cream cheese
1 tablespoon reduced-calorie
    margarine
3 tablespoons powdered sugar

20 bars

In medium mixing bowl, combine all bar ingredients, except walnuts and carob chips. Beat at low speed of electric mixer until moistened. Beat at medium speed for 2 minutes, scraping bowl occasionally. Stir in walnuts and carob chips. Spread into 9-inch square baking dish. Shield corners of dish with triangles of foil.

Place dish on saucer in oven. Microwave at 50% (Medium) for 6 minutes, rotating dish ¼ turn after every 3 minutes. Remove foil. Increase power to High. Microwave for 5 to 11 minutes longer, or until center springs back when touched lightly and no uncooked batter remains on the bottom. Cool completely on wire rack.

In small mixing bowl, combine cheese and margarine. Microwave at 50% (Medium) for 30 seconds to 1 minute, or until softened. Stir in powdered sugar until smooth. Spread icing over cooled bars.

Per Serving:			
Calories:	130	Cholesterol:	60 mg.
Protein:	3 g.	Sodium:	79 mg.
Carbohydrate:	28 g.	Calcium:	77 mg.**
Fat:	2 g.	Exchanges:	1½ starch, 1 vegetable

Whole Wheat Fig Muffins

1 cup skim milk
¼ cup vegetable oil
1 egg
1 egg white
3 tablespoons honey
½ teaspoon grated lemon peel
¾ cup bran flake cereal
⅓ cup chopped dried figs
2 tablespoons wheat germ
½ cup unbleached all-purpose flour
½ cup whole wheat flour
2 teaspoons baking powder

Topping:
4¼ teaspoons wheat germ, divided

17 muffins

In medium mixing bowl, blend milk, vegetable oil, egg, egg white, honey and lemon peel. Stir in cereal, figs and wheat germ. Let stand for 5 minutes. Add remaining ingredients, except topping. Mix just until dry ingredients are moistened. Line six muffin cups with paper baking cups. Fill each cup with 2 tablespoons batter. Sprinkle each with ¼ teaspoon wheat germ. Microwave at High for 2 to 3 minutes, or until tops are firm to touch, rotating cups once or twice. (Some moisture may remain.) Repeat with remaining batter and topping.

Per Serving:
Calories: 95
Protein: 3 g.
Carbohydrate: 13 g.
Fat: 4 g.
Cholesterol: 16 mg.
Sodium: 69 mg.
Calcium: 38 mg.
Exchanges: 1 starch, ½ fat

Gingerbread with Orange Sauce ▲

¾ cup unbleached all-purpose
   flour
½ cup whole wheat flour
½ cup reduced-calorie
   margarine
⅓ cup packed brown sugar
⅓ cup dark molasses
¼ cup fresh orange juice
2 eggs
1 teaspoon grated orange peel
¾ teaspoon ground cinnamon
½ teaspoon baking soda
½ teaspoon ground ginger
¼ teaspoon ground cloves
¼ teaspoon salt*

Orange Sauce:

½ cup fresh orange juice
1 tablespoon packed brown
   sugar
1 tablespoon reduced-calorie
   margarine
¾ teaspoon cornstarch
¼ teaspoon grated orange peel
⅛ teaspoon ground cinnamon

9 servings

In medium mixing bowl, combine all gingerbread ingredients. Beat at low speed of electric mixer until blended, scraping bowl constantly. Beat at medium speed for 2 minutes, scraping bowl occasionally. Pour batter into 9-inch square baking dish. Shield corners of dish with triangles of foil.

Place dish on saucer in oven. Microwave at 50% (Medium) for 6 minutes, rotating dish ¼ turn after every 3 minutes. Increase power to High. Microwave for 3 to 9 minutes, or until center springs back when touched lightly and no uncooked batter remains on the bottom. Let stand on counter for 10 minutes.

In 1-cup measure, combine all Orange Sauce ingredients. Mix well. Microwave at High for 1½ to 2½ minutes, or until sauce thickens and bubbles, stirring once or twice. Spoon 1 tablespoon sauce over each serving of gingerbread.

*To reduce sodium omit salt.

Per Serving:			
Calories:	219	Cholesterol:	61 mg.
Protein:	3 g.	Sodium:	240 mg.**
Carbohydrate:	34 g.	Calcium:	103 mg.**
Fat:	16 g.	Exchanges:	1 starch, 1 fruit, 2 fat

Poppy Seed Dinner Loaf

Vegetable cooking spray
1 tablespoon cornflake crumbs
¾ cup unbleached all-purpose
    flour
⅔ cup yellow cornmeal
2 tablespoons grated
    Parmesan cheese
1 tablespoon poppy seed
2 teaspoons sugar
2 teaspoons baking powder
¼ teaspoon onion powder
⅔ cup buttermilk
1 egg
1 egg white
⅓ cup vegetable oil

16 servings

Spray 8 × 4-inch loaf dish with vegetable cooking spray. Line bottom of loaf dish with wax paper. Spray wax paper with vegetable cooking spray. Sprinkle with cornflake crumbs. Tilt dish to coat. Set aside.

In medium mixing bowl, combine all remaining ingredients. Beat at low speed of electric mixer until moistened. Beat at medium speed for 2 minutes, scraping bowl occasionally. Spread batter evenly into prepared dish. Shield ends with 2-inch strips of foil, covering 1-inch of batter and molding remainder around handles of dish.

Place dish on saucer in oven. Microwave at 50% (Medium) for 6 minutes, rotating dish ¼ turn after every 3 minutes. Remove foil. Increase power to High. Microwave for 1 to 5 minutes longer, or until center springs back when touched lightly and no uncooked batter remains on the bottom, rotating dish once. Let stand on counter for 5 to 10 minutes.

Per Serving:
Calories:	92
Protein:	2 g.
Carbohydrate:	9 g.
Fat:	5 g.
Cholesterol:	18 mg.
Sodium:	68 mg.
Calcium:	31 mg.
Exchanges:	½ starch, 1 fat

Whole Grain Nut Bread ▲

Vegetable cooking spray
1 tablespoon wheat germ,
    divided
½ cup whole wheat flour
½ cup medium rye flour
2 tablespoons cracked wheat
    flour

2 tablespoons finely chopped
    walnuts
½ teaspoon baking soda
½ cup buttermilk
1 egg
1 tablespoon dark molasses

12 servings

Spray 1-quart round casserole with vegetable cooking spray. Sprinkle with 1½ teaspoons wheat germ. Tilt dish to coat. Set aside. In medium mixing bowl, combine whole wheat flour, rye flour, cracked wheat flour, walnuts and baking soda. Set aside.

In small mixing bowl, blend buttermilk, egg and molasses. Add to dry ingredients. Stir until blended. (Dough will be sticky.) Spread into prepared casserole, mounding slightly to form round loaf. Sprinkle top with 1½ teaspoons wheat germ.

Microwave at 50% (Medium) for 6 to 11 minutes, or until center springs back when touched lightly, rotating dish after every 3 minutes. Let stand on counter for 5 minutes. Cut into wedges. Serve warm.

Per Serving:
Calories:	70	Cholesterol:	23 mg.
Protein:	3 g.	Sodium:	48 mg.
Carbohydrate:	10 g.	Calcium:	31 mg.
Fat:	2 g.	Exchanges:	1 starch

Cran-Pineapple Bread

½ cup unbleached all-purpose
    flour
½ cup whole wheat flour
⅓ cup yellow cornmeal
1 teaspoon baking soda
¼ teaspoon ground allspice
¼ teaspoon ground mace
1 can (8 oz.) crushed
    pineapple, undrained
½ cup chopped fresh
    cranberries
¼ cup dark molasses
¼ cup reduced-calorie
    margarine, cut-up
1 egg
2 tablespoons chopped raisins

20 servings

Per Serving:	
Calories:	59
Protein:	1 g.
Carbohydrate:	11 g.
Fat:	3 g.
Cholesterol:	—
Sodium:	68 mg.
Calcium:	30 mg.
Exchanges:	½ starch, ½ fruit

How to Microwave Cran-Pineapple Bread

Line bottom of 2-cup measure with circle of wax paper. Set aside. In medium mixing bowl, combine all ingredients. Beat at high speed of electric mixer for 1 minute, scraping bowl frequently. Pour half the batter (about 1⅓ cups) into prepared measure. Cover with vented plastic wrap.

Microwave at 50% (Medium) for 6 to 10 minutes, or until center springs back when touched lightly and no uncooked batter remains on the sides, rotating measure ½ turn after every 3 minutes. Let stand on counter for 5 to 10 minutes. Loosen edges.

Invert onto wire rack. Repeat for second loaf. Cool completely. Cut two ⅜-inch slices from small end of each loaf. Set aside. Cut remainder of each loaf into 4 slices. Cut large slices in half.

Strawberry Banana Quick Bread

1 cup whole wheat flour
⅔ cup packed brown sugar
½ cup unbleached all-purpose
   flour
½ cup reduced-calorie
   margarine
⅓ cup buttermilk
2 eggs
1 cup sliced fresh strawberries
½ cup mashed banana
¼ cup finely chopped nuts
1 teaspoon baking soda
¼ teaspoon ground nutmeg

18 servings

Line bottom of 9 × 5-inch loaf dish with wax paper. Set aside. In large mixing bowl, combine all ingredients. Beat at low speed of electric mixer until moistened. Beat at medium speed for 2 minutes, scraping bowl occasionally. Spread batter evenly into prepared dish. Shield ends with 2-inch strips of foil, covering 1-inch of batter and molding remainder around handles of dish.

Place dish on saucer in oven. Microwave at 50% (Medium) for 9 minutes, rotating dish ¼ turn after every 3 minutes. Increase power to High. Microwave for 3 minutes. Remove foil. Microwave for 2 to 9 minutes longer, or until center springs back when touched lightly and no uncooked batter remains on the bottom, rotating dish once or twice. Let stand on counter for 5 to 10 minutes.

Per Serving:
Calories: 120
Protein: 2 g.
Carbohydrate: 18 g.
Fat: 8 g.
Cholesterol: 31 mg.
Sodium: 107 mg.
Calcium: 22 mg.
Exchanges: ½ starch, ½ fruit, 1 fat

Index